FIRST PRINCIPLES

&

FIRST VALUES

FIRST PRINCIPLES

&

FIRST VALUES

FROM EXISTENTIAL RISK TO EVOLUTIONARY LOVE

A NEW STORY OF VALUE FOR HUMANITY

. . .

One Mountain, Many Paths: Oral Essays
Volume Twenty-Five

DR. MARC GAFNI

Author: Gafni, Marc
Title: First Principles and First Values
Identifiers: ISBN 979-8-88834-035-6 (electronic)
ISBN 979-8–88834–052–3 (paperback)

© 2025 Marc Gafni

Edited by Talya Bloom and Elena Maslova-Levin

World Philosophy and Religion Press,
in conjunction with

IP Integral Publishers

https://worldphilosophyandreligion.org

JOIN THE REVOLUTION!

CONTENTS

CHAPTER TWO   THE FIRST PRINCIPLE OF THE INNATE PLEASURE OF TRANSFORMATION

CHAPTER THREE   **FIRST PRINCIPLES & FIRST VALUES: THE URGENT & ECSTATIC MORAL IMPERATIVE OF OUR TIME**

CHAPTER FOUR   **EVOLVING THE SOURCE CODE OF CONSCIOUSNESS AND CULTURE**

CHAPTER FIVE   SURVEILLANCE CAPITALISM: "WE'RE GOING TO STEAL YOUR EXPERIENCE WITHOUT YOUR PERMISSION"

CHAPTER NINE   EMERGENCE: CALLED BY MY FUTURE SELF

CHAPTER TEN   BEING PERSONALLY CALLED

CHAPTER ELEVEN   LANGUAGE AS A PORTAL TO FIRST PRINCIPLES

CHAPTER TWELVE   DIAGNOSING THE TECH PLEX: FROM DIGITAL DICTATORSHIP TO DIGITAL INTIMACY, FROM SOCIAL SELF TO UNIQUE SELF, FROM SOCIAL HIVE TO UNIQUE SELF SYMPHONIES

EDITORIAL NOTE ABOUT AUTHORSHIP, EDITING, AND THE RADICAL CONTEXT FOR THIS SERIES

ORAL ESSAYS FROM THE ONE MOUNTAIN, MANY PATHS WEEKLY BROADCAST

This volume is part of the Oral Essays library, a series of lightly edited, compiled transcripts of oral teachings given by Dr. Marc Gafni and the late Barbara Marx Hubbard in their weekly online broadcast, *One Mountain, Many Paths,* which they co-founded in 2017. Originally called an "Evolutionary Church," *One Mountain, Many Paths* became a key venue for the articulation of an inspired and deeply grounded new Story of Value in response to the meta-crisis. Marc and Barbara—together with Zak Stein,[1] Kristina Kincaid, Ken Wilber, Sally Kempton, Lori Galperin, Aubrey Marcus and dozens of other thought-leaders over the years—began to articulate what they call a World Philosophy and World Religion[2] as a context for our diversity.

---

1   Zak, together with Ken Wilber, has been Marc's primary intellectual partner and an initiate lineage holder in CosmoErotic Humanism.
2   This project is grounded in four core organizational frameworks: 1) The Center for World Philosophy and Religion, co-founded by Marc Gafni, Zachary Stein, Sally Kempton, and Ken Wilber, and chaired over the years by John P. Mackey, Barbara Marx Hubbard, Aubrey Marcus, Gabrielle Anwar and Shareef Malnik, Carrie Kish and Adam Bellow, and Kathleen J. Brownback. 2) The Office for the Future, chaired by Stephanie Valcke and Ivan Bossyut. 3) The World Philosophy and Religion Press, founded and chaired by Aubrey Marcus, together with Marc Gafni and Zachary Stein. 4) The Foundation for Conscious Evolution, founded by Barbara Marx Hubbard and currently chaired by Peter Fiekowsky. For a complete list of key leadership, see the Office for the Future website, www.officeforthefuture.com.

Until Barbara's passing in 2019, she and Marc transmitted teachings together as evolutionary partners and "whole mates," weaving together insights and transmissions from their decades of practice, study, teaching, and activism into a synergy of wisdom, a grounded vision for future policy across all sectors of society.

Much of the *Dharma* material below comes directly from Marc, so it was originally all in quotation marks—but that looked a little odd. So per his suggestion we removed them, and the reader should consider the paragraphs on the next several pages as one extended quote from him. We are joyfully grateful to Marc for the clarity of his *Dharma*, the elegance and "second simplicity" of this language, and the mad, Outrageous Love with which he transmits his teachings.

Barbara and Marc called the mission of *One Mountain* "a Planetary Awakening in Evolutionary Love Through Unique Self Symphonies." We are an evolutionary community with a deeply grounded, radically alive, and "post-tragic" revolutionary spirit. We are activating a new humanity and awakening as a new species: *Homo amor*, the fulfillment of *Homo sapiens*.

One Mountain is committed to articulating a Story of Value that can become the ground for the new society that must be birthed in response to the meta-crisis. We recognize that we are living at a pivotal moment in history. In this "time between stories," the great moral imperative is to tell the new Story of Value. It is ours to do, personally and collectively, with great trembling and ecstatic joy.

FROM DOGMA TO *DHARMA*: ETERNAL AND EVOLVING FIRST PRINCIPLES AND FIRST VALUES

The teachings are grounded in decades of deep study across many wisdom traditions. Over the years, week by week, these teachings were incrementally developed within the framework of the *One Mountain, Many Paths* broadcast. We often refer to these teachings as *Dharma*.

This word was originally used in lineage traditions to refer to something like universal law. This is a crucial realization: just as there is universal law in mathematical value, there is also a sense of universal law in ethics and value.

Historically, *Dharma* often devolved into unchanging dogma. Evolution was ignored, and the natural process of *Dharma* evolution became disconnected from its deep, eternal context. The weakness of the word *Dharma* is that too often it did not include the evolving insights of the sciences, it confused local cultural truths with universal truths, and it used words like "eternal," as in "eternal Tao," as opposed to words like "evolution."

Eternal came to mean unchanging, and that kind of thinking often led to overly ethnocentric readings of *Dharma*. Local systems would claim their religious and cultural insights as immutable, which stood in the way of the emergence of a genuine world Story of Value that is real, inherent to Cosmos, and backed by the Universe—even as it is also always evolving.

Or, as we often say, "eternal value is evolving value. The eternal Tao is the evolving Tao."

We have shown that, emergent from profound insights in the "interior sciences," eternal does not mean unchanging in time; it means what we call the deeper Field of ErosValue that is beneath culture, geography, and history, which lives beneath all individual and collective values, and beneath time and space itself.

As such, we have gradually transitioned from the term *Dharma* to the term *Value*, in the sense of the Field of Value that lives beneath all values. This Field of Value discloses as First Principles and First Values embedded in a Story of Value.

Indeed, as the interior sciences knew and the exterior sciences imply, Reality arises in a Field of ErosValue in which an entire set of mathematical, musical, molecular, moral, and mystical values are the very ground of all being. That Field of Value is eternal—the true ground of the Good, True and Beautiful—even as it is evolving.

But of course, it is equally critical not just to talk about evolving value, but to ground the evolving value in its true nature, the eternal Field of First Principles and First Values, always reaching for ever-more life, ever-more love, ever-more care, ever-more depth, ever-more uniqueness, ever-more intimate communion, and ever-more transformation.

As such, when we refer to the word *dharma*, which still appears in these texts together with the word value, we refer to an evolving *Dharma* grounded in an *eternal and evolving* Field of Value. Indeed, eternity and evolution are two faces of the whole, opposites joined at the hip, that characterize the nature of our Cosmos in virtually all of its expressions.

It's in these terms that we ground a robust world philosophy that integrates the validated, leading-edge insights of premodern traditional wisdom, modern wisdom, and more recent postmodern insights, weaving them together into a new whole greater than the sum of its parts.

This new whole is a shared Story of Value rooted in First Principles and First Values that are both eternal and evolving.

These First Principles and First Values of Cosmos are woven together into a new Story of Value as a context for our diversity, a new Universe Story. This new Story gives us the best possible responses we have to the mystery, and to the great questions:

- ◆ Who am I? Who are we?
- ◆ Where am I? Where are we?
- ◆ What should I do? What should we do?

It is only through such a shared Universe Story—a narrative of identity and ethos as a context for our blessed diversity—that we can realize how what unites is so much greater than what divides us.

Only a new Story of Value will allow us to both respond to the meta-crisis and participate together in birthing the most true, good, and beautiful world that we already know is possible.

THIS ORAL ESSAYS SERIES IS AN ENTRYWAY TO THE GREAT LIBRARY OF COSMOEROTIC HUMANISM

This Oral Essays series is part of the overarching project of the Great Library at the Center for World Philosophy and Religion, led by Dr. Marc Gafni, together with Dr. Zak Stein. The aim of the Great Library project is to articulate a robust and comprehensive new Story of Value, CosmoErotic Humanism, in the form of dozens of well-researched and extensively footnoted academic works.

Our vision is to provide the philosophical framework that will be vital for navigating humanity through this time of immense crisis and transformation.

To begin your journey into CosmoErotic Humanism, we tenderly refer you to the book *First Principles and First Values*, co-authored by Marc Gafni, Zak Stein, and Ken Wilber, under the name David J. Temple. David J. Temple is a pseudonym created for enabling ongoing collaborative authorship at the Center for World Philosophy and Religion. The two primary authors behind David J. Temple are Marc Gafni and Zak Stein, and for different projects, specific writers will be named as part of the collaboration, such as Ken Wilber and others.

Three other volumes complete this introduction: *A Return to Eros*, by Marc Gafni and Kristina Kincaid; *Your Unique Self*, by Marc Gafni; and *Education in a Time between Worlds*, by Zak Stein.

We hope that the Oral Essays in this volume, with their informal style of transmission, will serve as an allurement and entryway for you into the more formal books of the Great Library that provide the robust intellectual underpinnings of the new Story of Value.

A NOTE ABOUT THE EDITORS

This Oral Essays collection has been edited by students of the new Story of CosmoErotic Humanism. Each of us has actively participated in *One Mountain, Many Paths*, and most of us have been in deep "Holy of Holies" study with Dr. Marc Gafni for many years.

We have been privileged to find ourselves well-versed in the teachings, and even emerging as lineage-holders of CosmoErotic Humanism.[3]

We view this editing project as a privilege and a deep practice of study and clarification. We experience ourselves as a *mystical editing society*, frequently meeting and conversing together about the content—the depth of knowledge and wisdom offered here—as well as the technical intricacies involved with publishing a beautiful and coherent series of books. In so doing, we function as a "Unique Self Symphony," which itself is a Dharmic

---

3 CosmoErotic Humanism is a world philosophical movement aimed at reconstructing the collapse of value at the core of global culture. Much like Romanticism or Existentialism, CosmoErotic Humanism is not merely a theory but a movement that changes the very mood of Reality. It is an invitation to participate in evolving the source code of consciousness and culture towards a cosmocentric *ethos* for a planetary civilization.

The term CosmoErotic Humanism, initially coined by Dr. Gafni and colleagues, points to a complex, multi-faceted, layered, and nuanced evolutionary set of insights that has evolved over decades of intensive research, teaching, and spiritual practice from deep within a wide range of wisdom traditions (including the Wisdom of Solomon lineage tradition, Bodhisattva Buddhism, and Kashmir Shaivism), as well as multiple disciplines including complexity theory, chaos theory, emergence theory, molecular biology, and the more classical disciplines of the humanities.

The seeds of CosmoErotic Humanism were planted with Dr. Marc Gafni's work on a two-volume, 1,000-page opus called *Radical Kabbalah* (Integral Publishers, 2012). This scholarly work, sourced from deep study within the esoteric lineage texts of the Wisdom of Solomon, points to a non-dual, or acosmic, realization which—unlike the prevailing conceptualization of non-duality—does not efface the human being; rather, it is highly humanistic in its nature. The next step in the evolution of CosmoErotic Humanism was the insight that all of Reality is evolving Eros, which lives in, as, and through the human being.

A failure of Eros leads inexorably to the creation of narratives of "pseudo-eros." CosmoErotic Humanism is a response to the modern mental and social breakdown sourced in the proliferation of multiple forms of pseudo-eros and its broken narratives, such as rivalrous conflict governed by win/lose metrics and the dogmatic denial of intrinsic value in Cosmos, which together generate our current "global intimacy disorder."

term that connotes an omni-considerate collaboration between realized Unique Selves synergizing our unique gifts into a new emergence greater than the sum of the parts. Even as we worked diligently to standardize our editing styles, meeting on a weekly basis to debate the nuances of phrasing, we also operated from within a deep appreciation of the unique style that each editor brought to his or her work. As such, the reader might notice some variation in editing style among the books.

Please note that Dr. Marc Gafni has not reviewed these edited Oral Essays, as he is deeply engaged in writing the formal books of the Great Library. But he has been generous in responding to questions and providing overall guidance in the project. Overall, as Marc's students and students of the *Dharma*, we have made it a key project at the Center to publish these pieces of work relatively independently.

OUR UNIQUE ORAL-ESSAY EDITING STYLE PRESERVES THE ENERGY OF THE ORIGINAL TRANSMISSION

Dr. Marc Gafni is a uniquely gifted teacher whose oral transmission is imbued with a quality that has proven transformative for his students. Many of us feel mystically transformed by both the content and the underlying energy of the transmission style. Therefore, as we like to say, *trust the magic ways the Dharma comes through your unique understanding!*

As Marc's empowered students, colleagues, and beloved friends, we have a deep knowing that these teachings are vital for the survival and thriving of humanity as we know it, and we recognize the importance of publishing his teachings in a written format that will be accessible by future generations. At the same time, we sought to preserve the Eros of the original oral transmission with all of its nuance, power, and depth.

Our intention in the editing process, to the greatest extent possible, has been to keep these spoken artifacts intact in order to maintain the flow of the original transmission. We have therefore chosen not to engage in intensive formal editing, as we found that doing so resulted in the loss of the energetic transmission that is so key to fully receiving the *Dharma*.

After experimenting with many ways to present these texts, we developed a specific way of laying out the text on the page. Marc, in collaboration with Zak Stein and Russian intellectual/artist Elena Maslova-Levin—and ultimately all of the editors, through many conversations—developed a unique, artistic presentation of the text, using bolding, italics, bullet points, and other stylistic features which together serve to accentuate the immediacy of the oral transmission.

As part of this editing style, intended to preserve the integrity of the original transmission, we have refrained from removing the frequent recapitulations of key themes. We found that each recapitulation contributes something vital to the rhythm and music beneath the words, like the beating drum of our hearts.

These recapitulations not only review previous material but also add important new emphases, perspectives, and elements of the new Story of Value. We ask for your patience as a reader to trust the rhythm of these texts, and we trust you as a reader to have the depth and steadiness to find your way through.

KEY COMPONENTS: LINK TO THE ORIGINAL BROADCAST, EVOLUTIONARY LOVE CODES AND PRAYER

To supplement the written word, each episode includes a QR code linking to the original broadcast on YouTube, as well as occasional links to featured songs and video clips.

Each episode also centers around an "Evolutionary Love Code," formulated by Marc. These codes are part of the ongoing articulation and distillation of the *Dharma* as it unfolds and emerges, week by week, over the course of many years, through the mystical process we call Outrageous Love or Evolutionary Love.

Another core component of the *One Mountain, Many Paths* episodes is what Marc and Barbara called "Evolutionary Prayer." Prayer is experienced in *One Mountain* not in the old fundamentalist sense of a "cosmic vending-machine god" who is alienated from Cosmos.

Marc refers to this as the "god you do not and should not believe in"—and he often adds, "the god you don't believe in does not exist."

GOD IS THE INFINITE INTIMATE

In fact, in the *Dharma* of CosmoErotic Humanism, a new name for God has emerged: the "Infinite Intimate," who appears in first-, second-, and third-person expressions. Marc first shared this name as he heard it whispered in 2023, although earlier intimations and formulations of the name appeared as early as 2010.

In first person, God is infinitely alive and as intimate as our own first-person experience.

In second person, God is the infinitely intimate Personhood of Cosmos that knows our name and holds us—the God about whom we say, *whenever we fall, we fall into Her hands.* This is the God who is our Beloved, Father, Mother, Lover, and Evolutionary Partner.

Finally, in third person, God inheres in all of the First Principles and First Values of Cosmos, and in the laws of science (both interior and exterior) that govern manifest Reality.

Therefore, we have a realization of God as not only the Infinity of Power but also the Infinity of Intimacy.

In *One Mountain, Many Paths*, we are reclaiming prayer at a higher level of consciousness. And we are reclaiming prayer as deep, alive, loving, and intimate conversations with God as the Infinite Intimate who knows our name.

THE INVITATION

We invite you to find your way into this revolution. Each one of our Unique Selves and unique gifts are desperately needed as we co-create this new Story of Value together, as part of the covenant between generations, for the sake of the whole.

Let's *play a larger game* and evolve the very source code of consciousness and culture together.

With mad love,

The Editors

LOVE OR DIE

LOCATING OURSELVES: ARTICULATING THE ESSENTIAL CONTEXT FOR THE ONE MOUNTAIN, MANY PATHS ORAL ESSAYS

SETTING OUR INTENTION

Intention setting is everything.

We're here—as da Vinci was with his cohort in the Renaissance—**to play a larger game, to participate in the evolution of love, which is to tell the new Story of Value rooted in First Principles and First Values.**

- ◆ Our intention is to recognize the critical historical juncture in which we find ourselves.
- ◆ Our intention is to take our seat at the table of history and to say, *we take responsibility for this.*
- ◆ Our intention is to participate as revolutionaries for the sake of the whole.

What we're here to do is revolution; revolution for the sake of the evolution of love.

It's a revolution for the sake of the trillions of unborn lives that will not manifest:

- The unborn loves
- The unborn creativity
- The unborn goodness
- The unborn truth
- The unborn beauty

All of it looks to us.

Not because we're engaged in grandiosity. Not at all!

- We're trembling before She.
- We're trembling with joy at the privilege.
- We're trembling with joy at the responsibility.
- We're trembling with joy at the Possibility of Possibility.
- We have to enact a new Story in this moment of time. Because it is only a new Story that can change the vector of history.

The most revolutionary act that we can do—the greatest moral imperative of this time—**is to articulate a new Story at this time between worlds and this time between stories**.

Story is not made up, as postmodernity suggests. **We all live in inescapable frameworks; our framework is the story we live in.** Right now, Reality lives according to win/lose metrics, a story that is generating existential risk. **We need to change that story.**

When we change that story, when we tell a new Story—not a made-up story, but a new Story of Value, rooted in First Principles and First Values—**then it all changes.**

We need to participate in the evolution of the source code of consciousness and culture, which is the evolution of love.

It's the most important, exciting, evolutionary, revolutionary act that we can do to alleviate suffering: to be lovers.

Like Rumi, the great poet of Sufism, we have to be "mad lovers," because it's the only sanity.

To be mad lovers is to see around the corner, to not be so obsessed with the details of the contractions of my life.

Let me see bigger.

Let me take complete care of myself in every possible way, let me completely attend to those in my circle of intimacy and influence, and then—*let me expand my circle.*

That's what we're here for.

- Our intention is to participate in the *LoveForce*, the *LoveIntelligence*, the *LoveBeauty*, the *LoveDesire* that literally animates Cosmos all the way up and all the way down.
- Our intention is to participate in the evolution of love.

[*In the next few pages we will cover some key concepts which are essential to locating ourselves and setting the context for all the One Mountain, Many Paths Oral Essays. —Eds.*]

OVERVIEW: EROS IS NO LONGER A LUXURY—IT'S LOVE OR DIE

Eros is life.

The failure of Eros destroys life.

Our lack of Eros is poised to destroy the world.

All civilizations have fallen because the stories that they lived in were, in some sense, stories based on rivalrous conflict governed by win/lose metrics. Every civilization was weakened by interior polarization caused by the lack of a shared Story of Value.

We now have a global civilization, but we haven't created a shared Story of Value.

We haven't solved the generator functions that caused all civilizations to fall. Our global civilization has exponential technologies and extraction models depleting the Earth of resources that took billions of years to create, which is going to lead to a civilizational collapse.

Existential risk is risk to our very existence.

The choice is clear: love or die.

It's that simple.

Eros is no longer a luxury. It is an absolute necessity for the survival of the individual and the planet.

In the last half a century, modern psychology has documented an age-old truth: a fully nourished baby who is not held in loving arms will die.

So too, our world, both personal and global—even with all the resources of intelligence and technology at our disposal—will die without being held in love, in the embrace of Eros.

We must embrace a personal path of love and a global politics of love.

Not ordinary love. Not love which is "mere human sentiment," but Eros, or what we sometimes call Outrageous Love, which is the heart of existence itself.

We live in a world of outrageous pain.

The only response is Outrageous Love.

WHAT IS EROS?

Eros is the experience of radical aliveness, moving towards, seeking, desiring ever-deeper contact and ever-greater wholeness.[4] Eros is the core fabric of Reality's being and the motivational architecture of Reality's becoming.

Eros is what animates the evolutionary impulse itself, from the very inception of Cosmos all the way to our very selves, who awaken to the realization that the evolutionary impulse throbs uniquely in each of us.

The realization of human awakening and transformation that lies at the core of the interior sciences is the invitation—or even the urgent and desperate demand—of a madly loving Cosmos animated by infinities of power and infinities of intimacy.

The demand—the desperate invitation, the plea, the tender and fierce command of Cosmos that lives inside every human being—is to awaken: to awaken to our true nature as unique incarnations of Eros and Ethos that are needed and desperately desired by All-That-Is. Said slightly differently: Reality is Eros. Or: God is Eros.

The failure of Eros destroys life. The collapse of Eros is always the hidden (or not so hidden) root cause for the collapse of ethics.

This is true both personally and collectively. We live in a moment of a worldwide and personal collapse of Eros. Our lack of Eros is poised to destroy

---

4 We define Eros through what we refer to as the Eros equation (one of a series of what we call interior science equations):

> *Eros = Radical Aliveness × Desiring (Growing + Seeking) × Deeper Contact × Greater Wholeness × Self Actualization/Self Transcendence (Creation [Destruction])*

There are good reasons for the formal language of the interior science equations in these writings, and the reader is invited to explore them on their own, in particular, in our work, David J. Temple, *First Principles and First Values: Forty-Two Propositions on CosmoErotic Humanism, the Meta-Crisis, and the World to Come* (World Philosophy and Religion, 2024).

the world. Humanity is currently experiencing what has come to be known as existential risk, a risk to our very existence, or what I will refer to as the Second Shock of Existence.

EXISTENTIAL RISK: THE SECOND SHOCK OF EXISTENCE

The first shock of existence is the death of the human being—the realization that we will die, which dawns in human consciousness at the beginning of history. We are not talking about the biological fact of death but the *existential* realization of death. Although the interior sciences disclose that death is a portal between two days (there is vast empirical,[5] philosophical,[6] and anthro-ontological evidence[7] for the continuity of consciousness[8]), death is also, in our own direct surface experience, a stark end. And that is obviously not a bug, but a feature in the system.

---

5   We refer to evidence gathered by the most serious of researchers, beginning with Henry and Edith Sedgwick at Cambridge University and William James at Harvard University, and continuing in highly rigorous form for the last 150 years, as recapitulated by Whiteheadian scholar David Ray Griffin in multiple volumes. See also, for example, Dean Radin, *Real Magic: Unlocking Your Natural Psychic Abilities to Create Everyday Miracles* (Potter/TenSpeed/Harmony, 2018), *The Conscious Universe: The Scientific Truth of Psychic Phenomena* (HarperCollins, 2010), and other books. Or see the earlier classic by Frederic William Henry Myers, *Human Personality and Its Survival of Bodily Death* (Longmans, Green, 1907).

6   This requires a cogent analysis of materialism and dualism, and the introduction of the far more cogent third possibility, which we have called "pan-interiority."

7   We discuss Anthro-Ontology in some depth in *First Principles and First Values*, and see also the fuller conversation in David J. Temple, *First Principles and First Values: Towards an Evolving Perennialism: Introducing the Anthro-Ontological Method*—both published by World Philosophy and Religion Press, in conjunction with Integral Publishers. For now, we will simply define it as an "innate and clear interior gnosis directly available to the human being."

8   See Dr. Marc Gafni and Dr. Zachary Stein's essay in preparation, "Beyond Death: Anthro-Ontology, Philosophy, and Empiricism." This essay is slated to appear in the book *Towards a World Religion: Homo Amor Essays*. The essay is also the ground for a larger book by the same authors, *Twelve Portals to Life Beyond Death: Responding to the Second Shock of Existence*, in which we discuss three forms of material: the empirical, the philosophical, and the anthro-ontological, and show how each form discredits the notion of death as the end.

Our first-person experience is that death ends this life. It is not the *totality* of our experience if we go deeper inside, but it is obviously intended to be the central, potent, and painful dimension of every human life. Indeed, as Ernest Becker potently reminded us, the denial of death is at our peril.

All the stories and all the plotlines and all the threads of living end at that moment. Whatever happens beyond, we have an actual experience of ending. **Paradoxically, that ending, the experience of the finality of mortality, is what presses us into life.** From the implicit demand of the first shock of existence, human beings were activated and pressed into creative emergence, and what emerged was all of human culture, both interior and exterior.

The second shock of existence is the realization of the potential death of all humanity. After all the stages of human history—matter, life, and mind in all of their stages of evolutionary unfolding—we have come to this place in the evolution of humanity, in which the gap between our exponentially expanding exterior technologies and our stalled (or even regressing) interior technologies of value has created dire catastrophic and existential risks.

This gap generates extraction models and exponential growth curves, rivalrous conflicts based on win/lose metrics, tragedies of the commons, and multipolar traps, in which everyone has to keep producing to the nth degree, including weaponized exponential threats to our very existence because we are afraid that the other parties are going to do it and not be transparent—hide it from us and then dominate us.

GENERATOR FUNCTIONS FOR EXISTENTIAL RISK

Let's outline clearly the main *generator functions for existential risk*.

Rivalrous conflicts governed by zero-sum, win/lose metrics. Rivalrous conflicts generate extraction models at the core of the economic system and exponential growth curves. Both of these drive and are driven by a contrived system of artificially manufactured desires and needs, delivered into culture by ever more precise forms of micro-targeting to individuals and groups through the ever more immersive environment of the internet.

Next, rivalrous conflicts and exponential growth curves animated by win/lose metrics generate **complicated, fragile world systems** highly vulnerable to myriad forms of collapse. Fragile local systems are made exponentially more fragile on a global level by our inability to meet global challenges with social, legal, political, economic, and ethical infrastructures that remain largely local.

All of this is a direct result of the failure to develop more adequate interior technologies that would be sufficiently compelling to displace "rivalrous conflict governed by win/lose metrics" as the motivational architecture for the human life world.

This failure has led to the conditions that will cause the implosion of systems that are already and quite literally on the brink of collapsing themselves. That's what we mean by the *second shock of existence.*

To recapitulate: the second shock of existence is not the death of the human being, but the potential death of humanity.

It is the *Death Star* moment of our species.

THE DECONSTRUCTION OF INTRINSIC VALUE

We stand in this moment poised between utopia and dystopia, at a time between worlds and a time between stories. We need a new Story of Value, eternal yet evolving, rooted in First Principles and First Values, which would become a universal grammar of value and a context for our diversity.

This is exactly what the Renaissance was. It was a time between worlds and a time between stories. In the Renaissance, we had recently been challenged by the Black Death, a pandemic that swept across Europe. The

Black Death destroyed between a third to half of Europe and a huge part of Asia. People died horrifically, brutally, in the streets. They had no idea how to meet this challenge, and so, in response to the Black Death, da Vinci and Ficino and their cohorts understood that they had to tell a new Story of Value.

That story was the story of modernity. Did they get it right?

- They got part of it right, which birthed, to use Jürgen Habermas' phrase, "the dignities of modernity," such as new ways of gathering information and universal human rights.
- But they also deconstructed the source of Value. They lost the basis for the Good, the True, and the Beautiful.

The basis used to be divine revelation: *God told us.* But this claim was owned by religion, and every religion began to overreach and over-claim. The revelation was thus often mediated through cultural categories and wasn't fully accurate.

Modernity threw out revelation, but was unable to establish a new basis for value.

Value was just assumed to be real. As it says in the founding document of the American Revolution: *We hold these truths to be self-evident*—that is, *we don't really have a basis for value; we just take it as a given.*

In other words, modernity took out a loan of social capital from the traditional world. The source of value was never worked out.

And then, gradually, value began to collapse.

- The Universe Story began to collapse.
- The belief that the Good, the True, and the Beautiful are real began to collapse.
- The belief that Love is real began to collapse.

As Bertrand Russell is reported to have said, "I cannot see how to refute the arguments for the subjectivity of ethical values, but I find myself incapable of believing that all that is wrong with wanton cruelty is that I do not like it."

What do you do if you grew up in a world in which value is not real? A world without a source of value, without a Universe Story, without a story of human identity, without a story of desire, without a narrative of power?

In the words of W.B. Yeats, *the center does not hold.*

- You have a collapse at the very center of society, because you no longer have Eros.
- You no longer have a Reality in which value is real, and so you have this lingering sense of emptiness.
- You have a complete collapse at the very center.
- We become *the hollow men and the stuffed men*, gesture without form.

And that's the source of our current existential risk.

THE DEEPER ROOT CAUSE OF THE META-CRISIS: A GLOBAL INTIMACY DISORDER

Above, I have outlined the major generator functions of existential risk. But there is a deeper cause for the existential risk that lurks underneath the rivalrous conflict governed by win/lose metrics and the fragile systems they engender.

And we cannot take the Death Star down without discerning and addressing this. We have already alluded to this root cause above, but at this point we need to make it more explicit so that, from this context, the adequate root response will become clear.

Modernity threw out the revelation, but was unable to establish a new basis for value.

This ostensibly surprising statement can be understood in a few simple steps:

1. All of the catastrophic and existential risk challenges we face are global: from climate change to artificial intelligence, pandemics, systems collapse, and exponential arms races.
2. Every global challenge self-evidently requires a global solution.
3. Global solutions can only be implemented with global co-ordination.
4. Global co-ordination is impossible without global coherence.
5. Global coherence is only possible if there is a global resonance between the parts.
6. Global resonance is only possible if we have global intimacy.

ONLY A SHARED STORY OF VALUE CAN GENERATE GLOBAL INTIMACY

Global intimacy—just like intimacy in a couple—is only possible when there is a shared story.

Not just a shared history, but a shared Story of Value.

- It is only a shared global story that can generate a new emergent quality of intimacy: global intimacy.
- A shared Story of Value must be rooted in shared ordinating values, or what we have called evolving First Values and First Principles.
- Intimacy requires a shared grammar of value as a matrix for a shared Story of Value.

The global intimacy disorder is the root cause for existential risk. The global intimacy disorder underlies the core generator functions for existential risk.

The global intimacy disorder is rooted in the failure to experience ourselves in a field of shared intrinsic value. This failure derives from the deconstruction of value.

Indeed, it is wholly accurate to say that **the root cause of the two generator functions of existential risk is the failed story of intrinsic value, or what we might also call the breakdown of Eros.**

1. The first generator function is **the success story**. Our modern success story is rivalrous conflict governed by win/lose metrics, which violates all the terms of the Intimacy Equation: there is no shared identity and no mutuality of recognition, feeling, value or purpose, and instead of *relative* otherness, there is *alienated* otherness. Such a story generates complicated fragile systems with no allurement or intimacy between the parts, systems which optimize for efficiency (as an expression of win/lose metrics) and not for resiliency and life.

2. The second generator function is **the deconstruction of intrinsic value** itself. The deconstruction of value is the sense that human value does not participate in the intrinsic value of the Real, for the Real is dogmatically declared to have no intrinsic value. Thus, there is no shared identity between the interior of the human being and Reality. There is no common participation in a field of shared intrinsic value. Instead of being intimate with value, we are alienated from value. And only intrinsic value can arouse will: political, moral, and social will.

To sum up, without a shared grammar of value there is no global intimacy, and therefore no global coherence, and no global coordination in response to catastrophic and existential risk, which means, put simply, there will be, quite literally, no future.

HEALING THE GLOBAL INTIMACY DISORDER
REQUIRES THE EVOLUTION OF INTIMACY

But we are not hopeless. On the contrary, we are filled with great hope. Hope is a memory of the future. That memory of the future *is* the direct hit that takes down the Death Star, the culture of death. **The direct hit must be**—as it has always been in history—**the emergence of a new stage of evolution.**

Crisis is an evolutionary driver, and every crisis is, at its core, a crisis of intimacy: from the oxygen crisis of the single cells dying which generated multicellular life at the dawn of existence, to the existential risk in this very moment.[9]

The direct hit is therefore structurally self-evident: the evolution of intimacy itself.

What is intimacy, as a structure of Cosmos all the way down and all the way up the evolutionary chain? We engage this inquiry in depth in other writings, but for now we will simply adduce what we have called the "Intimacy Equation":

Intimacy = shared identity in the context of [relative] otherness x mutuality of recognition x mutuality of pathos x mutuality of value x mutuality of purpose

Intimacy is about the capacity of parts to generate a *shared identity* while retaining their otherness, or distinct identity. This requires multiple mutualities, including recognition, pathos (or feeling), value, and purpose. The parts must recognize and feel each other, even as they share value and purpose. But all of this must lead to intimate union—and not pathological

---

9 We demonstrate this principle in some depth in the multi-volume series, *The Universe: A Love Story* (forthcoming) (https://worldphilosophyandreligion.org/early-ontologies), *The Intimate Universe: Global Intimacy Disorder as Cause for Global Action Paralysis* (forthcoming), and in other writings of CosmoErotic Humanism.

fusion, where the distinct identity of the parts disappears—like subatomic particles that successfully become an atom, or two people who successfully become a couple.

THE DECONSTRUCTION OF VALUE IS THE DECONSTRUCTION OF INTIMACY

We have identified the global intimacy disorder as the root cause of existential risk. But the underlying ultimate failure of intimacy is the deconstruction of value itself.

The deconstruction of value means that human value does not participate in any sense of intrinsic value of the Real. This is not about individual *values,* but about *the Field of Value* that underlies all of them. **When the human being**—moved, often sincerely or even nobly, by myriad cultural, historical, and psychological confusions—**claims to have stepped out of the Field of Value, then intimacy itself is deconstructed.**

The deconstruction of value is the deconstruction of intimacy.

In the absence of a shared Story of Value, a story that is an authentic expression of Reality's Eros, a story rooted in *pseudo-Eros* takes center stage and becomes the generator function for existential risk. Our modern pseudo-Eros story is *rivalrous conflict governed by win/lose metrics.* Such a story catalyzes in its wake the second generator function of existential risk: *complicated fragile systems with no allurement or intimacy between the parts.* It is in that sense that we have argued that the first generator function for existential risk is the success story.

- The failure of intimacy is precisely the impotent experience that there is no shared identity between the interior of the human being and Reality. **There is no shared identity in the sense of any kind of common participation in a field of shared intrinsic value.**

- **But only a shared Story of Value can arouse the global will required to engage catastrophic and existential risk.** For it is only global political, moral, and social will—and we can even say *erotic* will—that can generate the most Good, True and Beautiful world that we have always known is possible.

THE EVOLUTION OF LOVE IS THE TELLING OF A NEW STORY

Coupled with the Intimacy Equation is the scientifically grounded realization, in both the exterior and interior sciences, that Reality is a progressive deepening of intimacies, or, said slightly differently:

Reality is Evolution. Evolution is the evolution of intimacy.

- The evolution of intimacy requires—both personally and collectively—a deeper, more accurate discernment of the nature of our universe, ourselves, and our beloveds.
- This new discernment generates a new global Story of Value.
- The new global Story of Value generates an emergent, heretofore unseen global intimacy and heals the global intimacy disorder.

The new Story of Value is the direct hit that takes down the Death Star and replaces it with the hope that invokes the memory of our best future.

Global intimacy facilitates global coherence, which facilitates global coordination, which activates the possibility of our creative and effectively coordinated global responses to the global meta-crisis in its entirety and its specific expressions.

To solve Bertrand Russell's challenge—the apparent argument for the subjectivity of ethical values—**we have to reground value theory in eternal yet evolving First Principles and First Values, and articulate a new Story of Value.**

This is what we call CosmoErotic Humanism.

CosmoErotic Humanism—together with other emergent strands—**needs to become the ground of a world religion as a context for our diversity**. We need religion, even as we need science, to articulate a shared global grammar of value.

As we said at the beginning, our choice is simple: love or die.

- To love means to participate in the evolution of love, which is the evolution of the human Story of Value.
- To love means to evolve and activate a new cultural enlightenment—rooted in a new narrative of identity, a new narrative of value, a new narrative of intimate communion, a new narrative of desire, a new narrative of power—all of which will birth new narratives of economics and politics.
- The evolution of love is the telling of a new Story.

The new Story that must be told is a love story, for in fact that is the deepest truth of Reality, rooted in the best exterior and interior sciences, that we have at this moment in time:

- Reality is not merely a fact. Reality is a story.
- Reality is not an ordinary story. Reality is a love story.
- Reality is not an ordinary love story. Reality is an Outrageous Love Story.

Story doesn't mean it's *made-up*.

It means doing the hard work of integrating the validated insights of the traditional world, the modern world, and the postmodern world.

This is the intention at the heart of telling the new Story of CosmoErotic Humanism.

ABOUT THIS VOLUME

We stand at a time between worlds, a time between stories—poised between dystopia and utopia. How we respond will have consequences and reverberations for many generations. *First Principles and First Values* offers both the most compelling diagnosis and the most effective—and indeed joyful—response to the looming threat of existential and catastrophic risk.

The core diagnosis is a "global intimacy disorder." This intimacy disorder is generated by and expressed as the modern success story which is the dominant narrative in virtually all of worldwide culture. The success story pits us against each other in rivalrous conflict governed by win/lose dynamics. This in turn generates what systems theory refers to as complicated or fragile systems which are optimized for short-term profit and efficiency rather than long-term resilience and depth.

Living in this pseudo-story, we are mis-aligned with Reality's deeper narrative arc and nature. We fail to see that we live in an Erotic Cosmos, and that intimacy constitutes all of Reality—all the way up and all the way down.

Intimacy—whether in a couple, a nation, or in the earlier worlds of biology and molecular coherence—is only possible when there's a shared Story of Value. At the molecular level, such a story is implicit in the scientific laws of Cosmos. At the human moral level, the shared story of value needs to be explicated and made conscious.

Intimacy expresses itself in the structure of conversation. Indeed, the interior and exterior as they are being currently unpacked in the oral and written teachings of CosmoErotic Humanism, demonstrate that we live in a "conversational Cosmos." Conversation is the core second-person experience that constitutes the context for all exchanges of Eros, intimacy, and love. Love is real, and one face of love is always conversation, all the way down and all the way up the evolutionary chain. All of Reality is animated by erotic conversation, form the molecular to the metabolic, from the mystical to the moral.

Love is real, and love is how Reality evolves. It's an inherent value of Cosmos, and as such constitutes the plotline of Reality. For the story of Reality is a love story—ever increasing and ever deepening *Eros Value* is the plotline of the cosmic story, from matter to life to mind.

Naturally, then, when that story breaks down, Reality itself breaks down. When Reality, at the human level of evolution, becomes so powerful that it determines the course of evolution—also known as the Anthropocene— then the human disassociation from the narrative arc of Reality's love story crashes Reality itself.

Once we realize that we exist in an intimate universe, we intuitively grasp— underneath all the important statistics and information—how a global intimacy disorder can generate existential risk.

To respond to the meta crisis, we must be able not only to *restore* premodern ethnocentric intimacies rooted in premodern visions of shared value or even the early modern intimacies of democracies, markets and liberal culture, rooted in implicit modern assumptions of value.

Rather, we need to *evolve* a new global intimacy rooted in First Principles and First Values which are the grammar for a shared language of value.

At the core, intimacy is rooted in a shared story, which itself implies shared *conversation*. As such, we begin to understand that the collapse of a shared Story of Value is core to the global intimacy disorder. Therefore, we must respond with the creation of a new Story of Value. The new Story of Value itself is a weaving together new sets of facts, in higher intimacy, from the both the interior and exterior sciences, and from every period of human history—premodern, modern, and postmodern.

Global intimacy begins with a vision of the CosmoErotic Universe, the Intimate Universe in which intimacy suffuses, constitutes, and coheres all of Reality—all the way up and all the way down.

Intimacy is a First Principle and First Value of Cosmos. And the evolution of intimacy—Cosmos reaching for ever deeper and wider values of intimate coherence—is a primary vector in the core plotlines of Reality. Intimacy is a subset of Eros and, like Eros, intimacy is an inherent value of Cosmos.

It's ErosValue reaching for progressively deeper intimacies that is the plotline of Reality—from matter to life to mind.

When that Story of Value breaks down, Reality itself breaks down.

As such, the only possible response must be the evolution of new structures of intimate coherence. Intimacy is rooted in shared value. As such only a new story of shared value—rooted in recognizable First Principles and First Values—has the capacity to generate the emergent possibility of authentic global intimacy.

Moreover, only with a clear set of universally recognized First Principles and First Values is it is possible to address the artificial intelligence (AI) value alignment challenge—in other words, *the existential need to upload a universal set of inherent values into AI which will generate ethical AI*. The book does not directly address this AI issue but it is rather part of the groundwork necessary to effectively engage the value alignment problem. At its core is the reclaiming of value itself—not as a dogmatic claim but as a deeper realization of Reality as a Field of Value governed by First Principles and First Values such as intimacy, Eros, relationship, and evolution.

This capacity to articulate a vision of ErosValue that is incarnate in us even as we participate in it is core to the transformation from *Homo sapiens* to *Homo amor*—the new human and the new humanity. It is only by articulating a new Story of Value that we can directly respond to the meta-crisis of our time.

We currently live in a world that does not recognize the possibility that First Values even exist. Under postmodernity, we view all Stories of Value as "social constructions," "fictions," or figments of our imagination—indeed such is the exact language used by popular postmodern historian Yuval Harari.

This collapse of the Field of Value is the ground that has allowed the "tech plex" to hijack our attention for profit, and to create forms of surveillance capitalism. Technology has become alienated from value because the moral theory at the core of technology dogmatically asserts that value is contrived. For example, basic human rights such as autonomy and freedom are assumed to be fictions or social constructions. Thus, the undermining of human freedom and free will is not considered to be heinous—for what can be wrong with undermining something that was never real in the first place. It's precisely such a deconstruction of the Field of Value that leads directly to one of two forms of existential risk: either to the death of humanity, or to the death of *our* humanity.

The basis for this new Story of Value, which we are calling "CosmoErotic Humanism," must be a response to the great questions of: *Who am I? Who are we?* We are neither skin-encapsulated egos or merely separate selves, nor are we only spiritual True Self or unity consciousness. Instead, we transcend and include both of those: we are each a Unique Self, an irreducibly unique individuated incarnation of the ErosValue of Cosmos, awake and alive in us, as us, and through us. The tech plex rejects human dignity and human personhood, and in doing so rejects the inherent value of our Unique Selves.

It's only once we come to see who we are that we can begin to tell a new a Story of Value and address the global intimacy disorder. We can begin the evolutionary re-inscription of First Principles and First Values back into the fabric of society and culture—and back into Reality itself.

Not only, however, are we Unique Selves, but we then come together to form larger "Unique Self Symphonies," in order to participate directly in the evolution of Reality, which is the evolution of love—aligned with the First Principles and First Values of Intimacy and Eros. These all comprise the motivational architecture of Cosmos.

As Unique Selves, you each have unique gifts to give. To give your unique gift, you must first be intimate enough with yourself to take your "unique risk," which only you can take. Once this happens, however, you become the intimate universe in person. The giving of your unique gifts is the intimate universe living in, as, and through you. You become the evolution of intimacy in person. Your transformation to ever deeper intimacies is the evolution of intimacy incarnate in your "sacred autobiography."

Reality has *telos*, a plotline, a narrative arc—towards ever greater connection. The interior of interconnectivity is intimacy. Intimacy co-evolves with creativity on a trajectory towards every greater wholeness, which itself is a movement towards every greater value.

The conscious participation in the evolution of intimacy, grounded in the realization that my true identity is *The Universe: A Love Story* in person, is the transformation from *Homo sapiens* to *Homo amor*, the new human and new humanity. Intimacy and evolution are both is experienced by *Homo amor* as a First Principles and First Values of Cosmos. The evolution of intimacy—or what might be expressed as the progressive deepening of intimacies—is realized by *Homo amor* to be the very plotline of evolution itself.

The most urgent need we have now is articulating this new Story of Value. We need to combine the best of the interior sciences (such as contemplation, meditation, and prayer) and exterior sciences (such as physics and biology). We acknowledge all the great wisdom from the premodern, modern, and postmodern eras—the gnosis which generated the dignities, rather than the disasters, of each of those expressions of consciousness—and weave them together into a new whole. This new Story of Value, grounded in a shared Field of Value itself, then becomes the "superstructure" upon which all the social and physical structures of the world are grounded.

In this way, a shared grammar of evolving First Principles and First Values comes to inform how we live—personally, interpersonally, collectively, and globally. It is only a new Story of Value that ever changes the direction of history. In this time between worlds and time between stories, it's only the articulation of an emergent post-postmodern Story of Value that will allow us to avert the myriad scenarios of dystopia and point us towards the more beautiful world we all know is possible.

When led by First Principles, we are responding to the call of our future selves, and to the unborn trillions who are all infinitely valuable and who desperately want to help evolve Reality and create new forms of intimacy and wholeness. We do this by listening to and clarifying our own unique "deepest heart's desires," which is another fundamental First Value of Cosmos. When we do this, we see that our desire is also the desire of the whole—and we see that need is synonymous with desire. As *Homo amor*, guided by a new Story of Value based in First Principles and Values, we are responding to the evolutionary need of Cosmos itself.

Volume 25

These oral essays are edited talks delivered by Marc Gafni between August 2020 and March 2024.

CHAPTER ONE

THERE IS NO RESPONSE TO EXISTENTIAL RISK WITHOUT FIRST PRINCIPLES

Episode 194 — June 28, 2020

LOVE IS REAL, AND LOVE EVOLVES REALITY

To ontologize love means to know that love is absolutely, totally real. It's not contrived. It's not made up. It's not a social construction of reality. Love is a quality of value. Its expression changes and evolves from generation to generation, but love is the most real force in Cosmos.

Love is what holds Reality together literally in every second.

Love is intelligent. We refer to God as LoveIntelligence, so love is intelligent. Love is also sometimes agonizing—so love is always a move between the agony and the ecstasy— but love is ultimately intelligent.

Love is moving:
- Towards ecstasy
- Towards depth
- Towards goodness
- Towards beauty

Love is not static.

1

Love is not just eternal; Love evolves. Love evolves Reality.

Reality is the story of the evolution of love. It's the story of the evolution of intimacy.

WHAT'S WORSE, THE JUMP TO 99% DESTRUCTION OR FROM 99 TO 100%?

One of the founders of the conversation around existential risk (meaning the very risk to our existence that we're faced with in this century), Derek Parfit, articulated this question.

Imagine you had three options:

- Option One: There's going to be peace.
- Option two: A terrible option is catastrophic risk, where pandemics are exponentialized. Ninety-nine percent of the world is destroyed.
- Option three: That extra one percent is destroyed. We go from losing **ninety-nine percent** of the population to losing 100 percent.

We're at this pivoting point. We're standing between utopia and dystopia, like in *Blade Runner, Hunger Games, Mad Max,* or *Avengers* in which there's a Thanos-like intervention. There are genuine dystopian visions.

I'm using popular culture to refer to genuine options being discussed actively today behind the scenes in the world. In *The Avengers*, Thanos destroys half of the world in order to solve the problem of overpopulation. The Avengers are superheroes who challenge Thanos, **but he makes a lot of sense, and the Avengers don't even have a narrative of value, a set of First Principles that allow them to challenge Thanos**.

The two final *Avengers* movies are about the superheroes taking on Thanos. Thanos is facing existential risk. He says the whole world is ignoring what's really going on and he decides to get the stones that will allow him to destroy half of the world's population, **to kill fifty percent of the population "for the sake of the larger good."** That's his moral equation. **The Avengers feel in their bodies that this is wrong, but they can't quite articulate why.**

There's this great battle that takes place. It's actually quite an important movie if you read between the scenes. It says more than even its creators intended—as is often true in popular culture.

Popular culture often reflects the deepest movements in the evolution of consciousness.

OPTION ONE FOR THE FUTURE: PEACE

Option one is that there's a genuine breakthrough, an evolution of culture and consciousness; we recalibrate Reality; we take Reality off of its self-terminating direction, off of its exponential growth curve, off of its extraction model.

But how are we going to do that? There's no ordinary path towards that.

- ◆ Derek Parfit didn't have a path.
- ◆ Nick Bostrom, who talks about existential risk, doesn't have a path.
- ◆ All the great derivative thinkers who talk around existential risk aren't presenting a path.

They're outlining the problem and sometimes offering piecemeal solutions. These are all important. **There are all sorts of things we can do, but they won't quite get us there.**

For example, in his new book *The Precipice,* Toby Ord talks about the Center for Biological Terrorism that's supposed to work to counteract bioterrorism in the world, and which has the same amount of staff (four people) and approximately the same amount of funding it would take to run a McDonald's—that's all. It's completely understaffed. So of course it's not going to do anything meaningful. So of course we need to up-level it to be able to be an effective organization. Those are important piecemeal things to do.

WHICH IS WORSE, THE MOVE FROM OPTION ONE TO TWO, OR TWO TO THREE?

Ord is a student of Derek Parfit, who was his doctoral adviser. Again, Parfit asks: which is worse, the move from option one to two or two to three?

One to two is from peace to losing **ninety-nine percent** of the population.

Two to three is losing the extra few people from **ninety-nine percent** to 100 percent.

Parfit makes the brilliant point that although it's counterintuitive, from a certain perspective the move from option two to three is much worse than from one to two.

Everyone assumes it's the other way. Everyone says, "Losing **ninety-nine percent** of the world is obviously far worse than just losing a few more people."

But stay close to this. I want to really feel this with you.

- ◆ It's so deep.
- ◆ It's beyond profound.

- It's beyond gorgeous.
- It's what keeps me awake at night.
- It keeps me awake during the day.
- It gives me energy when I have no energy.

This is why we're here. When you go from two to three, when you lose the last one percent, what have you done? **When you go from losing ninety-nine percent to 100 percent of the population, you lose *all* future generations.**

That's what Thanos in the *Avengers* movie was doing. He starts with destroying half the world in the second-to-last movie, and in the latest movie he says, "I'm going to destroy the whole thing and we're going to start again," in an attempt to destroy all future generations.

When you destroy all future generations, you're destroying:

- Every future soul
- Every future love
- Every future beauty
- Every future truth
- Every future possibility

It's taken us thousands and thousands of years. There are 10,000 generations of human beings.

WE HAVE COLLECTIVE RESPONSIBILITY TOWARDS FUTURE GENERATIONS

There's a covenant between the generations. As we've said before, **there is no collective guilt, but there is collective responsibility.** Every generation is responsible for its evolution of consciousness, which is the evolution of love. **But we're not an ordinary generation.**

We're at a phase shift the likes of which the world has never seen before. We're at a new moment in history.

The possibility of existential risk, that is, to go from wiping out ninety-nine to 100 percent of the population—the last 1% is gone, everything is gone—destroys all future generations.

We've finally arrived as a civilization to a point of excellence:

- To the gorgeous emergence of the feminine.
- To the place of voting and the beginnings of democracy, which is barely working as it is.
- To the place of this understanding of universal human rights.
- To the place that we can move Reality forward by knowing how to have a conversation with each other.
- To the place where we don't judge people based on the color of their skin, but by the content of their character. We're not doing identity politics. It's not about the tribe only. We've moved beyond the tribe to the nation.

THE RWANDA GENOCIDE HAPPENED BECAUSE THERE WAS NO NATIONALISM

Who knows about the Rwanda genocide? How many people know seriously about the Rwanda genocide?

In 100 days, 800,000 people were killed, but not by guns. How'd they get killed? Machetes, that's right, machetes. Why did that happen? Apologies to the liberal world here. **It happened because there was no nationalism.**

When we cry out against nationalism in the world, we actually don't quite understand it.

Nationalism means there's a nation. And the nation is beyond the tribes. What's happening now is that we're starting to see this retribalization where we're losing the nation. We're going back to the tribes: Brown tribes, Yellow tribes, Black tribes, Jewish tribes.

Of course there is gorgeous legitimacy to my unique identity. I've got my Unique Self instrument in the Unique Self Symphony. **Tribes are important. But tribes have to be part of the nation.** If the Hutus and the Tutsis had been part of a unified Rwandan nation as opposed to being separated by ethno-nationalism—meaning if they had nationalism, if that evolution of consciousness had taken effect—then that whole massacre might never have happened. Wow!

Then, in the evolution of consciousness, nations become part of a larger global communion of evolutionary souls. There's got to be a larger global communion.

But this whole set of ideas we're talking about, these are all new. We haven't gotten there yet. We're just at the beginning of this great experiment where humanity can unfold the most gorgeous truth, beauty, and utopia on Earth, levels of God consciousness, levels of Divinity. **We can literally participate as infinity intended.**

WE ARE THE MORE GOD TO COME

We as finitude literally participate in the evolution of God. We literally participate in the evolution of value. There's more value, and we can make more God-ness in the world. That's one of the deepest structures of the interior sciences in the lineage that we're unfolding here: **Infinity loves—** says William Blake—**the productions of time. Infinity loves finitude, and there's some way in which Infinity becomes more through finitude.**

+ In other words, manifestation—Reality—isn't an accident. It wasn't just divine love. It was divine self-love. And we're part of that divine self-love.

7

Infinity individuates through each of us and then —mystically, mysteriously, it's interior science—Infinity becomes more: there's more God, there's more Goodness, there's more Truth, there's more Beauty to come.

So if we go from peace to losing ninety-nine percent of the population, that's a horrific tragedy. It's catastrophic risk of the worst kind. But if we go from 99% to 100% existential risk, we've destroyed all of the futures, all of the God to come that's ours to manifest and to incarnate.

And we've violated the covenant between the generations. Ten thousand generations came before us. Each generation was a huge, momentous leap in consciousness. Sometimes it was the development of technological consciousness. A huge leap in, for example, human technology was clothing, human spacesuits that allowed us to inhabit different parts of Earth. Information technology came much later: infotech, biotech, and nanotech in our present moment.

- But there's been this gap. There's been this increase in *exterior* technology but the increase in interior technology hasn't kept pace, especially in the last 200 years.

In the last 200 years, after the great leap of the Renaissance—the great leap in exterior technology, the great leap of the story of modernity—**there's been a lagging, a collapsing of the evolution of interior technology.**

THE NEW STORY HAS NOT YET BEEN TOLD

We haven't integrated the new sciences and the old sciences, exteriors and interiors. We haven't told a story that's equal to our power.

So as the atom bomb exploded in 1945, and my beloved evolutionary partner Barbara asked President Eisenhower, "What's the meaning of our power?" He replied, "I don't know, young lady."

- We don't have a story of our power.

- We don't have a narrative of power.
- We don't have a narrative of identity.
- We don't have a universe story.

When you read Nick Bostrom—blessings, Brother Nick, you're doing awesome work—and Toby Ord—who's also doing a fantastic job—*there's no story*. When you listen to people like my colleague Sam Harris, you hear great information, but there's *no story*.

What's missing is what we want to call First Principles that come together and cohere as a new Story. First principles are what we've called *dharma*.

WHAT ARE FIRST PRINCIPLES?

First principles are the best integration of all the validated insights in all the streams of wisdom in the traditional, premodern period, meaning up until the Renaissance, all the great traditions of premodernity, all the deep spiritual traditions. These are validated insights based not on dogma but on deep experimentation in the interior sciences. Those shared insights of all the great wisdom traditions come together with the insights of modernity, roughly from the Renaissance until the 1960s—modern science, molecular biology, evolutionary science, systems theory, and complexity theory.

First principles are the integration of all the validated insights from every valid stream of wisdom:

- The premodern period
- The modern period
- The postmodern period

This is something my colleague Jordan Peterson misses. He says postmodernism is the source of all evil. Not quite. Postmodernism has very important insights.

- We gather those insights.
- We weave them together.

- We swallow it whole.

We weave the parts together into a new whole, a new configuration of intimacy. Parts come together as a new whole, and that new whole is the new Story.

THE NEW STORY MUST BE BASED ON FIRST PRINCIPLES

In the entire conversation around existential risk, around the serious challenges of today, there are no First Principles.

A colleague of mine wrote the other day, "We need to coexist with all the inanimate world, and we need to coexist with the animate world, and we need to coexist with each other."

Thank you. What does that mean?

- You can't coexist without First Principles.
- You can't coexist without a shared story.
- You can't coexist without a shared narrative.

LET'S IMAGINE A DIFFERENT SCENARIO TOGETHER

Can we imagine together? Can we use our imagination?

The human being is Adam. Adam means ground and Adam means imagination. The human being, Adam, is both Adam and Eve together in the original traditions, not man or woman. It's the original human being.

In the original Hebrew, the word for human being is the ground, *adama*, and also *di'mayon*, meaning imagination. Adam means imagination.

We're *Homo imaginus*. So let's dream. Let's imagine.

I want to imagine with you a scene that you didn't see. I was dreaming about this scene all day yesterday. Here's what didn't happen. Let's imagine what didn't happen and bring it into being.

It's December 2019 and you flip on CNN and Fox News or pick up the newspaper *Der Spiegel* in Germany. You flip on channels all over the world and you realize there's a global summit. It's before Christmas, maybe on Christmas, December 2019. All the world leaders have gathered. Based on advanced tracking technologies which have been funded (these technologies have not been funded, they're not available yet, but they could be, they've just been ignored), which allowed us to immediately sequence new viruses that are unknown to us, **we actually are completely aware that the Covid-19 coronavirus is on the way.** All the world leaders have gathered, and they shake hands, because we can still shake hands at that moment.

They literally hold hands and say, "Wow, we're one world."

Can you imagine that? Can you see that?

It's Christmas Day, 2019.

- We're one world.
- We're one love.
- We're one heart.
- We're one humanity.
- That which unites us is so much greater than that which divides us.

Each of the leaders gives a short talk and a blessing. They've been together for two days and on Christmas Day they say, "A pandemic is approaching, and we've got this. We're going to align with Mother Nature. We understand that the pandemic doesn't stop at individual states in the United States, and it doesn't stop at the border between Belgium and Holland, and it doesn't stop at the Germany border. It doesn't stop in Asia, and it doesn't stop in

Wuhan." **What this pandemic reminds us is that we're one world and one heart and one love**.

The pandemic is holding no-boundary consciousness. So what are we doing?

- We're ramping up our hospitals.
- We're preparing masks.
- We're going to share resources.
- We're going to stand together as the world never has in the history of humanity.
- We're going to stand together on the side of love.
- We're all on the side of love and we're standing against un-love, not against each other.
- We transcend ethnocentric consciousness.
- We expand our circle of intimacy.

In that moment something fundamentally dysfunctional in Reality, this global intimacy disorder, is healed in a way that it never has been.

It's like that moment when we saw a picture of the Earth from outer space and we realized *it was one world and one love and one heart.*

We see the global leaders together in our hearts and minds. Who can see this? Can anyone see this? Let's imagine this into Reality. We're *Homo imaginus*. We're literally going to make this true now. We're going to make this true.

I remember when I was growing up I saw an episode of the *Twilight Zone*, and there's this father who's a boxer—he loses the match, but then his son wishes that he had won, and he makes it true. The whole story is re-imagined backwards.

I can't promise you we can re-imagine this backwards, but this is a memory of the future. Let's be evolutionary mystics in this moment. Let's be evolutionary activists. We are the revolution.

AS EVOLUTIONARY ACTIVISTS AND MYSTICS, WE ARE ARTICULATING A MEMORY OF THE FUTURE

As mystics, we're articulating a memory of the future. Imagine that. It's a different world, isn't it?

Based on that, had we done that in the United States, we probably would have lost not 120,000 people, but maybe only 1,500. Wow!

Half a million people have died around the world—this is catastrophic risk—but none of them needed to.

And the economy is in shambles.

Just in the United States there are fifty million people unemployed, worried long-term about how to put food on the table. **That's what it means being concerned with the economy.** It's not concern for multinational corporations evading taxes. It's concern for people being able to put food on their table.

Can we feel that? We are those leaders. We actually are.

Now, what's missing? What doesn't get us there? We don't have First Principles. **The reason there was no meeting is that we don't have a Story of Value rooted in First Principles.**

A new story creates new global coherence, because a new story is a new configuration of intimacy. If we're not part of a shared story, we can't create global coherence.

What we just witnessed in the last four months is an utter failure of global intimacy, a global intimacy disorder writ large, which translated in an utter breakdown of global coherence.

- You can't evoke global coherence just by talking about existential risk.
- You can only evoke it by evoking a new Story.
- **And a new story has to be based on new First Principles.**

LET'S LET OUR LOVE CHANGE THE WORLD

What Parfit writes is that *if we survive this period, history is going to look back at this 100 years*—maybe it's these twenty years, maybe thirty, maybe ten, we don't know—but history is going to look back at this time, if we survive, and they're going to say:

- Those people stood up.
- Those people were heroes.
- Those people stepped out of the ordinary.
- Those people stepped out of the regular.
- Those people stepped out of the businesses they were running, trying to make their lives work.
- Those people stepped out of their narrow narcissism and their egocentricity which is all about: *What do I enjoy doing today?*

I love what you enjoy doing today, but you actually have privilege, sister. You have privilege, brother.

Let's love each other so much. The deeper we love each other, the more our love can change the world. The deepest and the most intimate levels we have that are hidden in the deepest places of Goddess's heart have to explode with each other.

It's got to be seen and acted on the stage of Reality. **Let our love love the world open.** That's who we are. That's our intention.

We do sensemaking, but not as a commentary on public events, and we're not just New Age spiritual inspiration or fundamentalist spiritual inspiration.

- We're weaving the new Story.
- We're articulating First Principles.
- We are the revolution.
- We have to be pure.
- We have to love each other.

It's all about the way we love each other and the way we love Reality open with radical activism.

LINES OF DEVELOPMENT THROUGHOUT HISTORY: TECHNOLOGY AND INTERIORS

What we're calling the first shock of existence is the experience, at the dawn of the human being, of our death. I confront my own death. Then we go through all the levels of consciousness, all the developmental levels of the human being. We go from stage to stage.

Do you know that writing began only 5,000 years ago? Writing is only 5,000 years old. There are 10,000 generations of human beings, and each one adds a link to the chain.

We go through all the technological levels, from hunting and gathering through early farming—horticultural with a handheld instrument—and then to the use of horses and oxen of various kinds. Then, we slowly go through different stages of more advanced kinds of farming. It goes on for quite a long time till we finally get to early modernity. We have this explosion in the Renaissance of the principles that brought the Industrial Revolution. Then we ultimately get to this larger Information Revolution, which turns into biotech and nanotech—and we're now at the dawn of artificial intelligence. **That's the technological line of development.**

There is also an interior line of development. In the interior line of development, we move from clans and their interior structures of consciousness, and then to the structures of consciousness of kingdoms.

- Initially we have clans.

- Then we have tribes. Tribes are defined by blood. Bloodlines define tribes. Race defines tribes.
- Then we move beyond race and bloodlines and beyond the racism implicit in them and we move to empires and nations.
- **In a nation the tribes are united.** It's a great leap in the evolution of love. The Hutus don't kill the Tutsis, because they're part of a greater nation. The tribal doesn't become my identification.
- Now we've got this notion of empire, this larger sense of identity, but we also have this new emergence in the Renaissance.

As the empires expanded, they ultimately seeded what would become the Renaissance, which is the emergence of worldcentric consciousness.

We move from clan-centric to a kind of ethnocentric tribe to an ethnocentric larger empire nation. Each one is more and more expanded ethnocentric circles of intimacy.

Now we move towards this emergence of universal human rights, this new understanding of the human being, the scientific method. This all explodes into Reality. **For the first time we can actually extrapolate universals from particulars.**

It's not just particular nations, which are expanded tribes merged together, and then each nation says, "I'm the best," or each religion says, "I'm the best and I've got to destroy the other ones." That notion of thinking goes on pretty much through World War I.

But already in the Renaissance the seeds of overcoming are planted. The seeds of universal human rights are planted. Although it takes time, it takes till after World War I and then really after World War II to fully move beyond it.

- There's the gradual emergence of worldcentric intimacy.

16

- There's the gradual emergence of a sense of universal human rights.
- There's the emergence of the feminine.
- There's the abolition of slavery, at least so it seems.
- There's this enormous move forward.
- There's a League of Nations.
- There's a United Nations.

There are these early steps, but they're based on very limited First Principles.

- What's the interior technology that's moving the world from the Renaissance till today essentially?
- What's the big momentous leap in this evolutionary story, this new emergence?
- What's the interior emergence of the Renaissance?

It's simple: separate self.

THE FIRST PRINCIPLE OF SEPARATE SELF LEADS TO THE DIGNITY OF MODERNITY

What does separate self mean?

The first principle of separate self is:

- I'm not defined by my tribe.
- I'm not defined by my race.
- I'm not defined even by my nation.

There's a notion of individuation, meaning you have irreducible value and dignity as you.

This is the notion of separate self. It's the dignity of separate self. **From the dignity of separate self comes emergent freedom, emergent dignity.** That's a momentous leap forward.

SEPARATE SELF BECAME ALIENATED FROM THE LARGER FIELD

What does this leap forward leave behind? **It leaves behind in the premodern period the realization that the great traditions had of True Self.**

This wasn't the popular realization, but **the most advanced, esoteric realization at the leading edges was this realization that *I'm one with the field of consciousness*.** Let's call that True Self.

Erwin Schrödinger, the quantum physicist who's describing the True Self realization, describes it as *the knowing of one mind, the singular that has no plural.*

The total number of True Selves in the world is one. *I'm one with the Field of Consciousness.*

In the leap to separate self in the modern world, that realization is lost.

Separate self emerges with this new dignity, and the premodern traditions got lost.

They were still there; they were still practiced; they were still at play.

But at the center of the leading edge of consciousness there was the sense that individual human reason and human rationality and the sense of reason per se could dominate. And the dualism of the seventeenth century between spirit and matter—where matter is dead and inert, while spirit is alive—gave way to materialism.

The top half, the top story of dualism, meaning spirit, got lopped off.

God was declared dead—because God was caricatured as the *god on a throne in the sky who created the world via fiat: deus ex machina.* That god was killed. But people didn't realize that God is so much deeper and more than that. People killed a caricature of God. What we had left was materialism, which believes that matter is dead and inert.

> *Now we have a sense of being separate Selves. We have dignity, but now we're not quite sure why we have dignity.*

The dignity started to be contrived, especially as the false Neo-Darwinist dogmatic claim was made that we're just a random aggregation of particles, that Reality has no purpose or *telos*, that it's not going anywhere, and that to even talk about *telos* is heresy.

FROM SCIENCE TO SCIENTISM: FROM DIFFERENTIATION TO DISSOCIATION FROM SPIRIT

It's not that science was bad. Science was doing something incredibly noble and beautiful. **Science was trying to liberate the ability to know from the shackles of the great religions.** The religions that told Galileo, "What you see through your telescope is not what you think you see."

Religion crushed the endeavor of human knowing outside of the realms of dogma. That was religion's great shadow.

At its very leading edge, religion was beautiful and had developed the consciousness of True Self, of knowing this oneness with the field of consciousness. **But an exoteric public religion crushed knowing.** So science wanted to liberate knowing—with the scientific method—from the shackles, the suffocating horror and cruelties of religion. Science liberated itself out of any connection to religion. Science differentiated itself from Spirit. **But then that differentiation became a dissociation.**

> *Science's differentiation from religion became a complete dissociation from Spirit.*

The separation of the value spheres of, let's say, religion and of, let's say, science, from interior morals—that separation became a dissociation.

19

THE TOP HALF OF DUALISM WAS LOPPED OFF, AND WE WERE LEFT WITH DOGMATIC MATERIALISM

This is a First Principle.

The separate self that began with this innate dignity, this innate assumption that the separate self was part of a larger Field—that assumption was lost.

The separate self became desiccated.

The separate self became kind of like a dangling modifier in a sentence of Spirit that was erased.

The separate self begins as an adjective and as a verb in a sentence of Spirit, in a uni-verse, a sentence of Spirit, a verse, *a verse which was one Universe,* one love, one heart. Then the separate self became a dignified expression. That was a natural intuition, but it was never expressed as a First Principle, it was taken as a given.

But then we started to talk about dualism, and we said that material was inert and dead, and that only spirit was real, and spirit lived in the human being.

And then the vision of Spirit/God was slaughtered, because that vision of Spirit/God was too connected to premodern superstition and, as Voltaire said, "remember the cruelties," and we were left with a denuded dualism. We just had its bottom half. What's the bottom half of dualism by itself? Materialism.

If you knock off the top half of dualism, what do you get? Materialism.

That's all you get: dogmatic materialism, which now dominates science. Science is afraid to say anything else. **What gradually happens is that science becomes as dogmatic as the religion it rebelled against.** Very often there's a revolution, and then the revolution becomes more oppressive than those people you're rebelling against. This happens a lot in politics.

THE RETURN OF SPIRIT IN THE TWENTIETH CENTURY

It's the nineteenth century and separate self is a desiccated separate self. It's what's called by the poet T.S. Eliot, "the hollow men and the stuffed men, paralyzed, gesture without motion." Wow! Or as Yeats says in his poem "The Second Coming," "The best lack all conviction. The worst are full of passionate intensity. Surely some revelation is at hand."

We've got this separate self, which is this new emergent story of modernity, but the dignity of the separate self has been undermined, denuded.

We just have this desiccated separate self, this dangling modifier in a sentence that's been erased, in a uni-verse that's no longer a verse in this larger text.

What happens next in the democracies around the world is that a new teaching begins to emerge. **The old premodern teaching of the East, the teaching of enlightenment, begins to emerge again. There is a revivification of mystic teachings.**

Swami Vivekananda, who appeared at the great world's fair back in 1893, was part of this revivification. **There's this reconnecting through a whole series of moves as this True Self tradition finds its way back into the Western world.** Aldous Huxley, who wrote *Brave New World*, writes a book called *The Perennial Philosophy*, which is about this tradition of True Self.

People such as my colleague and dear friend Ken Wilber, in the modern American context, picks up meditation, along with dozens and dozens of other teachers. For example, one of Ken's original teachers, Rudrananda, was also the teacher of my dear friend Swami Chetanananda. There's this entire explosion of Muktananda teachers, then you've got wilder versions of this with other teachers.

You've got this explosion of True Self all over the democratic world. Then it begins to move into places like Russia. It's all over the world, True Self.

It's not quite Indian philosophy. It's mysticism. It's the mysticism of the East and the West:

- It's Hasidism in the West;
- It's dimensions of Steiner in the West;
- It's Indian philosophy.

Indian philosophy is provocative, but it actually raises the entire deep mystical tradition—East and West—which is the True Self tradition.

It's this True Self tradition that's very strong, for example, in Hasidism. There's a book by Rivka Schatz called *Ha-Hasidut Ke-Mistikah* in Hebrew. In English it's *Hasidism as Mysticism*. Everyone should read it. The first three chapters are about this True Self tradition at the core of the Hasidic tradition. It's one of the major moves in Steiner. It's very important in Steiner.

The move of India towards the West provoked the West into re-accessing its own mystical traditions that it had put to the side. All of a sudden Meister Eckhart comes back in style—a Christian mystic who's also a True Self mystic. **True Self mysticism begins to dominate the field.**

The First Principle of Enlightenment begins to dominate.

People like Richard Alpert, a young Jewish kid from Boston whose dad was the head of the local Jewish organization, changed his name to Ram Dass. Another guy named Jeffrey Miller changed his name. You've got Surya Das and Ram Dass and Krishna Das, all Jewish boys, who all went East, hung out with Neem Karoli Baba. And then there's Jack Kornfield and Sharon

Salzberg and Joseph Goldstein and Danny Goleman. There's this whole gang who write and they're beautiful.

Ram Dass and I loved each other. We once spent an incredible nine days together. Then he came to meet me in L.A., and we spent this incredible day together. I shared with him what I'm about to share with you.

This re-embrace of True Self starts before the 1960s. It's popular in the 1960s, but it starts at the turn of the twentieth century. It really starts in the 1900s when it starts to get bigger and bigger and bigger. It's also rooted in theosophy, in Madame Blavatsky. The transcendentalists are very important, Wordsworth and that whole gang, as well as Walt Whitman, who's super important. There are multiple influences that come together— Alice Bailey and Gurdjieff are all part of it—and they explode this True Self vision into the West.

My original lineage is Hasidism, which is the Hebrew lineage of Kabbalah wisdom. In Hasidism, of course, there's a strong True Self tradition. While I was studying the True Self tradition in Hasidism, I was also expanding and studying the Three Wheels of Buddhism, Theravada and Mahayana and Vajrayana. I was also exposed to Kashmir Shaivism, which is completely gorgeous, through a number of people, and to particular worlds that Ken Wilber and I talked about. And I was exposed to readings in philosophy all across the board, particularly Fichte and Schelling, in terms of their visions of True Self. So I'm reading, reading, reading, and my body says, "No." My body says, "This is not enlightenment. This is beautiful, this is true, but it's limited."

I started talking to people about it. I talked to colleagues who—I won't mention the names—are each one of them the leading names today in the enlightenment world and I just say, "No, this is not quite right. This is true, but it's not right. My body tells me it's not true."

So they say to me, "That's your lack of realization. That's your ego hijacking it. You don't want to give up your ego."

The talk is about the impersonal. *You've got to move beyond separate self.* Separate self is the personal. *You've got to move beyond the personal to the impersonal.*

Ken Wilber describes in all of his early books True Self and views that as the ultimate accomplishment, the ultimate realization. But my body knew *that's just not right.*

- ◆ I went deeper and deeper into the lineage.
- ◆ I went deeper and deeper into my body.
- ◆ I went deeper and deeper into what the personal is.

I prayed and screamed and fought and yelled and argued and practiced.

And I began to realize and to formulate clearly—emergent from the lineages of Kabbalah but also emergent from an enormous amount of the sciences, and how the sciences define Reality—that we start with the personal of the personality and we get to the impersonal. We go from separate self to True Self.

We've got to leave behind that separate self that in the Renaissance became the center of everything. The great traditions weren't wrong. If I'm just the separate self of the Renaissance, the dignified individual, then *that dignified individual,* when you cut out Spirit, *becomes the hollow men and the stuffed men.*

- ◆ We've got to go back and reclaim True Self. That's absolutely true.
- ◆ But what the West did is that it reclaimed True Self and left separate self behind.

WE RECLAIMED TRUE SELF AND LEFT THE SEPARATE SELF OF THE ENLIGHTENMENT BEHIND

The entire movement of enlightenment reclaimed True Self but left behind the separate self that the Western Enlightenment had put forward. **The**

classical enlightenment traditions, mystical enlightenment traditions, East and West, left the separate self behind.

The separate self was the product of what we might call the Western Enlightenment. The Western Enlightenment, which started in the Renaissance, puts the separate self in the center and says *this is the dignity of the separate self.* So when we reclaimed True Self in Western consciousness, we left that separate self behind. The separate self was supposed to *die on the cushion.* That's what the teachers taught pretty much across the board.

The notion that the separate self has dignity was lost.

"You've got to use your relative self—which was the term they used for separate self—to navigate Reality, but basically the relative is just the relative. It's the Absolute where it lives and the Absolute is True Self."

I knew that wasn't true, and I knew that was a mistake. And pretty much everyone laughed. One person, a very well-known teacher today, said, "What Marc is doing is a desecration of the *dharma.*" People were furious. But you've got to stay loyal to She, you've got to stay loyal to realization, and gradually I was able to articulate the following.

FROM SEPARATE SELF TO TRUE SELF AND BEYOND

If we start with First Principles—and this is what enlightenment means—it means that we start with separate self. The separate self of the Western Enlightenment is really important, because the separate self of the Western Enlightenment is about moving beyond suffering. The separate self of the Western Enlightenment is the dignity of the individual.

Originally, the Western Enlightenment innately placed separate self in a larger frame, in a larger script of the universe but later got desiccated when dualism—which posited a split between spirit and body—became only materialism, so that separate self became the *desiccated hollow men and stuffed men* of the poet.

This original, healthy separate self is important, because the separate self is about moving beyond suffering.

But then we need True Self. The movement of consciousness was right. We need to bring True Self back because True Self is *also* about moving beyond suffering.

- The Western Enlightenment says, "to move beyond suffering you need to reify, you need to place at the center the dignified separate-self human being."
- Mystical enlightenment—both East and West, though it's usually identified only as Eastern Enlightenment—says, "No, to move beyond suffering you've got to get rid of your separate self and realize yourself only as True Self. Your separate self has to die on the cushion." You've got mystical Eastern Enlightenment, expressions of it in both the East and the West, which say to move beyond suffering, to heal yourself, and then to heal Reality, your narrative of identity has to be True Self. Separate self is an illusion.

But then you have the Western Enlightenment—the Renaissance through the Industrial Revolution, and the French Enlightenment—which says, "No, no, you cannot only define yourself in terms of larger contexts. You have independent, irreducible dignity. Only this separate self will take you beyond suffering."

Now we have two things that are called enlightenment: mystical Eastern enlightenment (as it appears East and West), and Western Enlightenment. And they both completely oppose each other.

That's what kept me awake night and day, because with that contradiction at the heart of culture we don't have a shared First Principle, we don't have a sense of identity, and I understood it's going to destroy culture.

So I prayed and practiced and began to realize the following. That's what the *Unique Self* book is about, and that's what the book *Self in Integral Evolutionary Mysticism* is about.

I began to realize the following. And we're about to get to a critical First Principle that changes Reality:

We need to distinguish between separateness and uniqueness.

WE NEED TO DISAMBIGUATE BETWEEN SEPARATENESS AND UNIQUENESS

Both the Eastern mystical enlightenment and the Western Enlightenment—the Western Industrial Revolution, French, Renaissance enlightenment—confused separateness and uniqueness, and that created this huge set of mistakes that can actually destroy culture. They're the source of our win/lose metrics with its extraction model, exponential growth, and its self-terminating nature that will destroy us. **We have to distinguish between separateness and uniqueness.**

The Western Enlightenment, the individual of the Renaissance, said, "Oh, you've got to be separate self. That's what you've got to be because separate self is the only source of dignity." And they got rid of True Self.

That's a mistake. That's not true. You're not just separate self—you can be Unique Self.

FROM SEPARATE SELF TO TRUE SELF AND UNIQUE SELF

What is Unique Self? Unique Self includes all of you. None of you is left out. It's not impersonal enlightenment. It's what we called back in 2002, "personal enlightenment."

- All of me is included.
- Particularly my uniqueness is included. *My uniqueness is not my separateness. I am a Unique Self,* meaning *I'm not separate self.*

The Western Enlightenment got it wrong in saying: "We need to be a separate self to have dignity." No. I can actually realize:

- I'm part of the Field of True Self.
- I'm one with the Field of Consciousness.
- I'm one with the Field.

And as we added later: *I'm one with the Field of Consciousness and Eros and Desire*—and **that Field of Consciousness, that seamless coat of the Universe is seamless but not featureless.**

- *I'm its unique feature.*
- *I'm a unique expression of the entire Field.*
- *I'm a unique emergent of the entire Field.*

So to be Unique Self means I'm not merely a desiccated separate self. I've reclaimed the Field of True Self.

Not as a dogma, but as the result of the best experiments in all the interior sciences that you can access directly. If you do the experiment yourself, you'll realize that *you are consciousness beneath your personality.* You can access that dimension of yourself in many ways. **I'm part of the Field of True Self, but I'm an irreducibly unique expression of that field. I'm Unique Self.** That's the correction of the mistake of Western Enlightenment.

But now we've got to correct the mistake of Eastern Enlightenment, which said, "You've got to be True Self and therefore you've got to give up all separation."

Eastern Enlightenment also conflated—confused—separation and uniqueness.

Text after text after text from popular Eastern Enlightenment texts— like *A Course in Miracles*, or like many texts all over the American spiritual community—**all conflated separateness and uniqueness.**

Many ancient texts conflated separateness and uniqueness. I've collected lots and lots of those texts, ancient and modern. You've got to disambiguate, to separate separateness and uniqueness. No, I'm not just separate self—I'm True Self, but **True Self doesn't obliterate my uniqueness.** I'm a unique expression of True Self. Actually, there is no True Self anywhere in the manifest world. **Every True Self is a Unique Self.** Wow!

Now Unique Self becomes the core structure of Cosmos.

FROM UNIQUE SELF TO EVOLUTIONARY UNIQUE SELF

The next step is that I realize that **Unique Self exists in an evolutionary context.** There's a larger evolutionary context at play.

I'm not just Unique Self—I am *Evolutionary* Unique Self. I am the first-person of evolution. I realize I am *uniquely* evolution. **I am the personal face of the evolutionary impulse beating in me, as me, and through me.**

EVOLUTIONARY UNIQUE SELF IS A UNIQUE CONFIGURATION OF OUTRAGEOUS LOVE

Now we've added this Evolutionary Unique Self, but that's not enough. Evolutionary Unique Self is a unique configuration of Outrageous Love.

- What is the interior experience of the evolutionary impulse?
- What is the interior experience of the Field of Consciousness?
- What does the Field of Consciousness feel like?

The Universe feels, and the Universe feels love. Not ordinary love, not love just between two separate-self human beings as expressed in the Renaissance, which then devolved into desiccated separate selves, *the hollow men and the stuffed men.* It's not ordinary love which is a strategy of the ego or a way to get status and security—which are of course legitimate—but that's not what we're talking about.

We're talking about Outrageous Love, the Eros that animates the Cosmos.

You begin to realize that True Self is not just a Field of Consciousness. That's a mistake. It's not just awareness. It's not just awareness of awareness. That's not going to take you home. Rupert Spira, love you madly, brother. It's not going to take you home.

The interior quality of the field is Eros, is Outrageous Love, is ananda.

When I say "I am evolution" I mean:

- I'm a unique configuration of Outrageous Love. Outrageous Love is the animating Eros of the evolutionary impulse.
- I'm a unique configuration of that animating Eros of the evolutionary impulse, which is moving towards the evolution of intimacy, the evolution of love. **I'm a unique expression of the evolutionary impulse that's moving towards the evolution of love.**

And as such, I realize that Outrageous Love moves through me.

We can all realize and access that First Principle:

- I'm a Unique Self.
- I'm a Unique Self in an evolutionary context.

- I'm a unique expression of True Self.
- I'm a unique expression of True Self in an evolutionary context, which means I'm Evolutionary Unique Self.

EVOLUTIONARY UNIQUE SELF IS *HOMO AMOR*

As Evolutionary Unique Self who am I? I'm *Homo amor.*

Homo amor means I am amor: love. But we've ontologized love, so love is my core identity.

My core identity is love, but it's *not ordinary love, not romantic love*— although romantic love might be an expression of Outrageous Love. **My core identity is the actual quality of Outrageous Love, which is personal.**

To recap:

1. Level one is personality: separate self.
2. Level two is the impersonal: True Self.
3. Level three is the personal beyond the impersonal.

Together with my dear colleague and gorgeous integral philosopher Ken Wilber, we argued about this material and went back and forth in 2002 and 2003 and 2004. Ultimately, I then wrote 1,500 pages about this lineage, which comes from an enlightenment lineage, and Ken read the whole 1,500 pages in a couple of nights and wrote me back, "Okay, I got it. I got it, man." He was in. He said, "This is a critical new enlightenment lineage that we have to integrate in the integral world." I wrote the *Unique Self* book in 2009, but began to present this in the world in 2004–2005.

THE EMERGENT REALIZATION OF UNIQUE SELF

In 2005, Ken gathered this group of teachers at what was then called the Integral Spiritual Center, and I was just delighted and honored he asked me to present this new enlightenment lineage called Unique Self.

Our colleague Genpo Roshi was there, Diane Hamilton was there, Sally Kempton was there, and other younger integral people were there. Sean Hargens and Terry Patten were there, Lama Surya Das was there, and a whole host of people from lineages around the world. Everyone was like, "What is this?"

There was enormous opposition to it in the one sense, and recognition in the other. Ken really loved it, and it was gorgeous. Then everyone began to get on board. **I called it Unique Self.** Unique Self was a word that had already existed in a book I'd written called *Soul Prints*, but Ken and I talked about it, and he said, "Let's take your Unique Self word and make that central."

Then a little short time later Terry wrote a book that had a chapter on Unique Self. He was gracious enough to recognize how we sourced it. Genpo Roshi wrote a book, and it had a chapter called Unique Self. **We put it into culture; we changed something together in the source code of consciousness. In the entire enlightenment community around the world this began to spread.**

Andrew and I still argued about it. Andrew Cohen and I still had major, public, knockdown debates on it. In the end, in 2011, the *Journal of Integral Theory and Practice* published an issue on this notion of Unique Self, which became a new chapter everywhere in integral theory.

This is not an integral theory issue. Integral theory is gorgeous. **But it's Unique Self theory. It's part of a broader CosmoErotic Humanism.** It's Unique Self theory. There's an integral scaffolding. Integral is meant, as Ken set it up, as a scaffolding. Integral theory is very, very important. I've sent a lot of people to integral theory.

Unique Self is the expression of this new emergent moment of consciousness. It's Evolutionary Unique Self.

That's what we mean by *Homo amor*.

HOMO AMOR IS THE FULFILMENT OF THE NARRATIVE ARC OF COSMOS

Homo amor is the realization that I'm a unique expression of the LoveIntelligence and LoveBeauty of Reality.

> *Evolutionary Unique Self, or Homo amor, becomes the fulfilment of the whole story.*

Unique Self is the next stage in the evolution of love. If you get the storyline, you get that there's a narrative arc to Cosmos, which is by itself a great realization. The dogmas of science don't see a narrative arc.

Cosmos moves from matter to life to mind.

First there's matter. People call it inanimate matter, but it's not inanimate— it's sentient, it's alive.

It's not materialism and dualism. Matter itself is inherently creative.

Then matter moves through all the stages, from the first nanoseconds of the Big Bang, to quarks to subatomic particles to atoms, differentiated into molecules, then into macromolecules that then intensify their intimacy and awaken as cells and then to multicellular structures, then to organisms and organs and all the way up to plants, fish, amphibians, animals, neural nets, neural cords, up to hominids walking on the savannah.

That's all life.

So it's matter, then the explosion of life. Matter is the physiosphere. That's the first Big Bang. Then matter fulfills itself in life.

MATTER TRIUMPHS IN THE FORM OF LIFE

Life goes through all of its stages till we get to hominids walking on the savannah. That's the biosphere. So the physiosphere, the first Big Bang, triumphs in the second Big Bang. The second Big Bang is life, the biosphere.

Then you go through all the levels of the biosphere. Then the biosphere/life triumphs in the human being. At some point there's this explosion, this momentous third Big Bang. The noosphere, the mind, the self-reflective mind is born.

Matter triumphs in life.

Life triumphs in self-reflective mind.

That's the third Big Bang.

Then we go through all the stages of the third Big Bang, through all the developmental stages of human history that we described. Then we get to a new set of First Principles.

We integrate premodern validated insights of all the wisdom streams, together with the modern validated insights of all the wisdom streams, together with the validated insights of all the postmodern wisdom streams. They come together and there's a fourth Big Bang, the fourth Big Bang is Unique Self. In other words:

The triumph of the self-reflective human is *Homo amor*.

Now, if you don't faint in rapture and ecstasy at the beauty, the elegance, the gorgeousness of what this human story is—this is the new universe story. This is the new *dharma*. These are the new First Principles. The new First principle is the Fourth Big Bang. In other words, in the third Big Bang we got as far as separate self, which birthed the dignities of modernity. But separate self dissociated from True Self and then True Self took the stage, so we just had this conflict between Eastern and Western Enlightenment. Western Enlightenment was all about separate self, dignity

34

of the individual. It said, *anything that effaces the individual is a cult, so let's get rid of those bad people.*

But actually that's not true. Cults are pre-personal. But there's actually a transpersonal option. *There's a personal beyond the impersonal,* and that actually is Unique Self.

Unique Self corrects the fracture in the misunderstanding of separate self.

It says separate self actually has to emerge and reclaim its ground as True Self. We're part of the Field of Consciousness, but that Field of Consciousness is not just consciousness—it's Eros, it's outrageous love, it's desire. I'm part of the Field of Eros, Outrageous Love, and desire, but I'm a unique expression of that field. That's the fourth Big Bang.

When I begin to actually experience myself as a unique expression, not as a theory but in my first-person lived identity—as a unique configuration of that field—then the third Big Bang has triumphed, mind has triumphed into *Homo amor.*

- That's the omega point.
- That's where we're going.
- That's the fourth Big Bang.
- That's what we've dedicated our lives to.

It's only the emergence of a new human and a new humanity that can actually generate the response to existential risk and to the second shock of existence.

So then around 2006–2007 this starts seeping into the world, little pieces of it, but each one is a little piece. So some people will get the notion, *okay, that uniqueness is part of it,* but they'll lose the evolutionary impulse, and other people will get the evolutionary piece but lose uniqueness. So in 2009 I actually wrote the *Unique Self* book to get this straight, but now we've got to issue a new version of the *Unique Self* book to actually integrate all the pieces as Unique Self theory.

Unique Self theory is not an abstract theory—it's the new story.

I am *Homo amor*. I am the new human. *Homo amor* is not just an individual human being—it's the new humanity.

HOMO AMOR: IN RESPONSE TO EXISTENTIAL RISK

This is the revolution. We're part of this revolution. We are the revolution of the fourth Big Bang. That's us.

It's only the fourth Big Bang that can respond to existential risk.

It's only the fourth Big Bang that can respond to artificial intelligence that obsoletes jobs and then obsoletes human identity as we know it.

- Without Unique Self, there's no game.
- Without Unique Self, there's no identity beyond my job.
- Without Unique Self, there's no reason why Thanos shouldn't— in the *Avengers* movie —wipe out everybody and wipe out the future and just start it again, because there's no dignity to the separate self.
- Without the irreducible dignity of the Unique Self, there are all sorts of solutions to existential risk which are tragic.

The irreducible dignity of the Unique Self is the separate self post True Self. The separate self, the ego self, is not wrong. It's not that you have to obliterate the ego, and it's not that you have to evolve beyond ego.

There's all this talk about evolving beyond ego. The people who talk about evolving beyond ego are the most dangerous, because you can't call them on their ego—they just deny it.

But you never evolve beyond ego. Your ego instead transmogrifies and transmutes into your Unique Self.

- Is there a danger of confusing Unique Self and ego? Of course there is, so you have to point out the distinction. In the *Unique Self* book, there are twenty-five distinctions between ego and Unique Self.
- Is there a danger of confusing True Self enlightenment with totalitarianism? Of course there is, but we don't dismiss True Self enlightenment. We have to distinguish.
- Unique Self is a higher individuation beyond ego.
- Then I participate in the Unique Self Symphony, which is why our vision, our goal, is a Planetary Awakening in Love through Unique Self Symphonies.

We come together as unique expressions of the self-actualizing Cosmos. We are unique expressions of the self-organizing Universe. **Each one of us is a unique expression of the self-organizing Universe, the self-actualizing Cosmos, and we each have outrageous acts of love to commit.** That is what it means to awaken as *Homo amor*.

In the consciousness of *Homo amor*, there's only one question. It's not quite the "Who am I?" of True Self, which is Ramana Maharshi's question, where the answer is "I am," meaning I'm the impersonal I-Am, impersonal consciousness. That's part of the ground, but it's insufficient. True Self is insufficient.

No, it's not just who am I.

It's *who am I and what's there to do*. What's the deepest answer to *who am I?*

THE PUZZLE OF *WHO AM I?*

What's *Homo amor*'s answer, which has to become part of my first-person consciousness? We democratize enlightenment, and we democratize greatness. The democratization of enlightenment has to be a kind of democratization of enlightenment where every person realizes in their first-person: *I'm a unique configuration of Evolutionary Love. I'm a unique configuration of the evolutionary impulse.*

♦ Separate self is a puzzle piece. But in the Western Enlightenment everyone thinks there's no puzzle, just the individuated I—that's all there is. *I'm a puzzle piece, but there's no puzzle*? **It doesn't work.**

♦ That's when we bring True Self back into Western consciousness and into the democratic world and all over the world. We bring it back and they say, "No, there is no separate self. There's just one puzzle, but it's all one." You say, "What about the lines separating the puzzle pieces?" Your enlightenment teacher tells you, "That's just an illusion."

So they're both crazy-making, because when you're looking for the puzzle as separate self and your teacher tells you there is no larger puzzle—the modern teaching of Hobbes' law—it's crazy-making. That's why you have mental breakdown happening all over the world, because **we're told a lie that violates our interior**.

But then you go to True Self, and we're told another lie or partial truth, which is that there's just the one piece of the puzzle. The lines separating the puzzle pieces: *that's all an illusion.*

♦ Then we actually deepen, and we realize—through the fourth Big Bang, Unique Self—that *there's a puzzle piece, and that the puzzle piece completes the puzzle.*

♦ Oh my God, so I'm held. I'm held by the larger puzzle, and I complete the larger puzzle.

♦ Then I go the last step, to Evolutionary Unique Self, and realize that I'm a puzzle piece that evolves the whole puzzle, *but that's me personally.* My personal love story is part of the Universe: A Love Story. **I am implicated in the evolutionary process.**

I am personally implicated. But by personally we don't mean the *merely* personal—we mean the personal *beyond* the impersonal. My love story is chapter and verse in the Intimate Universe, in the Universe: A Love Story.

It's a *uni*-verse again. It's one Eros and one love and one heart again, but a one which is *e pluribus unum*: the many that are the one. It's diversity and plurality together with unity at the same time. It's individuation within union.

The only mature individuation occurs in the context of a larger union.

WHO ARE YOU?

You are an irreducibly unique expression of the LoveIntelligence and LoveBeauty that is the initiating and animating Eros and energy of All-That-Is, that lives in you, as you, and through you, that never was, is, or will be again in all eternity other than through you. As such:

- ◆ You have an irreducibly unique perspective.
- ◆ You're an irreducibly unique quality of intimacy.
- ◆ Your irreducibly unique perspective and your irreducibly unique quality of intimacy come together to foster your unique gift. Your unique gift is your very being.
- ◆ Your very being-ness is your unique gift, and it's also a unique gift that only you have a capacity to offer. It's the unique activism that you can offer into your unique circle of intimacy and influence.
- ◆ You do this when you access your deepest heart's desire, which is the field of desire uniquely expressed as you, and commit your Outrageous Acts of Love.

- Your Outrageous Acts of Love that are a function of your deepest heart's desire, which is the field of desire and consciousness uniquely expressed as you.

It's actually you, the leading edge of evolution, you who manifested the whole thing, because where else could you have been at the Big Bang other than right there? There was no place else to be. You started the whole thing.

- Our hands are linked in Unique Self Symphony.
- Each of us is committing Outrageous Acts of Love.
- Each of us is standing together at the abyss of darkness and generating this fourth Big Bang, generating this Unique Self symphony.
- It's that set of First Principles that's going to take us beyond existential risk.
- It's that set of First Principles that's going to take us beyond catastrophic risk.
- It's that set of First Principles that are going to heal suffering, feed the hungry, realize human potential, realize hope beyond imagination, realize Beauty, Goodness, and Truth beyond imagination.

WITHOUT THOSE FIRST PRINCIPLES WE'LL FAIL

According to Toby Ord, over the next X amount of time, dozens or hundreds of years—he did all the deep mathematical work—we've got a one in two chance of making it over the long term.

So let me tell you something: **Without First Principles, we've got no chance.** With First Principles, we're going to take this all the way home and create a utopia on Earth unlike any you can ever imagine. Remember, that first elementary particle at the moment of the Big Bang that took us from quarks to culture, lives in you and lives in me and lives in us together.

That same generativity, that same creativity, that same love, that same Eros that took us from bacteria to Bach, from mud to Mozart, from dirt to Shakespeare—**that inherent *telos* of the ceaselessly creative Cosmos lives in us.**

Just like that first elementary particle had within it the capacity to manifest all that's most gorgeous, True, Good, and Beautiful, that elementary particle is literally in each of us.

All the interiors and exteriors live in us exponentialized, so we are the face of the new Divine, even as She holds us at the same time. Even as the Field of God is beyond us, it lives through us.

We are the leading edge, all of us together, and we together commit our Outrageous Acts of Love. We stand as a Planetary Awakening in Outrageous Love through Unique Self Symphonies.

- That's a First Principle.
- That's our basis.
- That's our foundation.
- That's where the revolution moves.

CHAPTER TWO

THE FIRST PRINCIPLE OF THE INNATE PLEASURE OF TRANSFORMATION

Episode 195 — July 5, 2020

ONTOLOGIZING LOVE AS AN EVOLUTION OF INTIMACY

The first thing we know is: *Amor—its insides are lined with love.*

That's not a declaration. **We're here to ontologize love. Love is not weak, love is strong.**

Meditation won't take you to love.

It's very important. I want everyone to get this. There's no good research that validates a direct, clear correlation between meditation and love. Meditation won't get you to love. It's one of its problems. Meditation will help you dissolve your sense of limited separate self, but it won't get you to love. **You have to *practice* love.**

This is very important.

You have to realize:

◆ That love is the heart of Cosmos itself.

43

- That the interior of Cosmos itself is built on allurement.
- And that Cosmos is the progressive deepening of intimacies.

That's a First Principle.

Now, again, are we aware of evil? Of course we're aware of evil. But you can't even say the word "evil" unless you realize that evil is a failure of intimacy. **We live in an Intimate Universe—it's intimacy from the very beginning**. From the first nanoseconds of the Big Bang with the mathematical principles all at play, unfolding all the way through the worlds of matter in all of its levels, then the worlds of life, then the world of mind. From the physiosphere: matter, to the biosphere: life, to the noosphere: self-reflective mind—**every one of those levels is an unfolding of a deeper intimacy, which means a wider, shared identity**. That's what an Intimate Universe means.

What is intimacy? This is a First Principle intimacy formula:

Intimacy = shared identity in the context of (relative) otherness

There is no *absolute* otherness; that's something that meditation helps you with, and so does chanting.

Intimacy = shared identity in the context of (relative) otherness + mutuality of recognition + mutuality of pathos (we feel each other) + mutuality of purpose.

That's true from subatomic particles all the way through molecular structures and cellular structures, all the way through plants, neural cords, neural nets, animals, and all the way up to hominids on the savannah, then all the way through all the stages of human history that are moving towards a progressive deepening of intimacies.

Now, as that happens, **as human power exponentially increases, the fringes of society based on distorted First Principles do too. They can cause enormous damage because we lose touch with the broader picture.**

- There's a progressive deepening of intimacies.
- We move towards greater unions.
- Exterior technologies get deeper and deeper.
- Interior technologies get deeper and deeper.
- We hit the Renaissance. The separate self emerges, along with universal human rights, the emergence of the feminine, the scientific method, this whole new intimacy with Reality—but *the story is flawed.*

It's a flawed story. It gets locked into separate self. It's locked into the sense of, *Okay, the separate self has dignity, but I'm just a separate self. I'm a monad in a mechanistic universe.*

That flaw in the story creates a distortion of First Principles.

We begin to operate in a success story according to win/lose metrics, which is the source of that flaw in the storyline, the source of every issue, every existential risk, we're facing today. So **we have to go back and ontologize love.**

TRANSFORMATION IS THE NATURE OF THE HUMAN STORY

Evolution is a series of transformations.

In the old vision of the world, God spoke, and the world appeared. Now, that's not the sense of the internal texts, which talk about not six days in the sense of six, twenty-four-hour days, but about six periods of time. There was no sun and moon till several days in, so obviously we're not talking about days. That's a huge mistake.

No, it's not talking about days. It's talking about this unfolding.

Major thinkers for 2,000 years hold that these are six unfoldings.

When you read the text carefully, it talks about *Tadshe ha'aretz deshe*: "Let the Earth bring forth grass," meaning there's an interior process of evolution.

Nonetheless, the exoteric/public position was that God waves a wand and Reality appears. It's not quite like that. If you read the mystery traditions carefully, and you read the modern mystery tradition of science—because science is the greatest mystery tradition we have, and we have to hold it that way—we realize that **Reality is actually a series of transformations.**

You start with the first nanoseconds of the Big Bang, from the first integration/differentiation, when the first elementary particles come together and create subatomic particles:

- The original matter differentiates as a subatomic particle.
- Then the subatomic particles come together and differentiate as an atom. These are transformations.
- Then atoms come together, and they differentiate as molecules, then molecules as macromolecules.

Each one of these is a complete transformation. It's a momentous leap. Each leap builds on the one before it. It's a series of transformations.

If you really get who you are, for real—you don't need poetry because science is poetry, and science is a mystery tradition—then you get that your particular transformation is literally, not figuratively, not metaphorically, in a direct line with all of the previous transformations from the moment of the Big Bang.

All constituent elements of reality, exterior and interior, actually live in you, meaning:

All exteriors live in you; all previous stages of evolution live in you.

- We're literally stardust.
- We're literally elementary particles. When we breathe in, we breathe in every breath that's ever been in reality (at least up to about two years ago). It's all in us.
- All interiors are in us.
- **All of interior consciousness lives in us.**

46

That's one of the realizations of practice. That's the interior sciences. So when I transform, my transformation is in direct line with the whole process, and my transformation evolves the whole process. It moves the entire thing forward. The whole thing moves forward. **My transformation transforms the whole thing.**

REALITY HAS A NARRATIVE ARC OF INTENTION

What's the one move we can make that will be a First Principle that removes jealousy, that removes the win/lose metrics, that removes competition?

What's the one world-uniting move in which literally, in one swoop, you remove competition, you remove jealousy, you remove the status seeking, you remove the win-lose metrics, and everyone becomes part of the same shared story?

What's the move? The move is the realization:

One—

- That growth and transformation is the nature of the human story.
- That the human story is actually a journey.

But not metaphorically!

- That the Cosmos *itself* is a journey.
- That the Cosmos *itself* is a story.

The dogmatic materialist side of science doesn't realize that.

The dogmatic side of religion doesn't realize that.

Religion said, "Reality is a hallway to lead you to the better world. That's what Reality is."

Science said, "Reality is a series of random facts," —not actually science but Scientism: the dogmas of science.

The deeper Reality both in Spirit and in science—the deeper, more esoteric traditions, the deep implications of a true reading of contemporary science and a true reading of the inner space of Spirit—**is that Reality is a story, it's a journey.**

That's actually, literally true, not metaphorically true. It's *literally* true.

Reality is a series of transformations.

Two—

+ Reality has a narrative arc of intention

It's going somewhere.

It has *telos*.

It has direction.

There's an inherent ceaseless creativity of Cosmos that has direction. It's a series of transformations.

Three—

+ My growth, my transformation is part of that story.

It's gorgeous. I'm so wildly excited to talk to you about this.

Four—

+ There's no competition, because the nature of growth is *I have to grow from where I am.*
+ We all have our unique starting point for our journey of transformation. We're born into that unique starting point, and we have to transform from there.

- At this moment in my life, my success is based on my ability to accomplish my transformation. **My Unique Self transformation is not in relation to you; it's in relation to me.**

By definition, my success is: Within the context of my life and my lineage and my life story, have I transformed?

You've got to transform in the context of your Unique Self journey, your lineage, your family history, your gorgeousness, your rapture, and your wounds.

All of it, it's yours to transform.

None of it is an accident.

There's an arc of intention in Cosmos.

You were born because Cosmos intended you to be born in a particular place, in a particular time, to a particular set of parents, with a particular social context.

And there's great mystery.

Five—

- We've got to begin to be responsible for each other's journey. In other words, I've got to begin to realize my Unique Self is not my separate self.
- We're in a Unique Self Symphony.
- We're responsible for each other. There's collective responsibility.
- We stand together.
- We rise together; we fall together.
- **We can't just be in our journey. We're responsible for each other's journey.**

So our metrics of success are twofold:

- ◆ A— Did I accomplish my transformation?
- ◆ B— Did I stand for your transformation?

Did I realize my transformation? There's no competition between me and you.

Did I stand for your transformation? We call that Unique Self Symphony. We call that a planetary awakening in love through Unique Self Symphonies.

That's a set of First Principles. Wow!

WE PLACE OUR ATTENTION TOGETHER

When we come together and we place our attention on each other, we move from the rational to the *ratio*, the source of the word "rational." We're in music together. When we place our attention, something happens, something opens up. It's not the old premodern guru function, which is so easily subject to abuse, and which we don't believe in—

We believe in a Unique Self Symphony in which the next Buddha is the Buddha and the sangha. There can be individual Buddhas with their Unique Self genius, but we're part of a sangha, we're part of a Unique Self Symphony.

When we come together and we place our attention together, that is where the First Principles break open.

Imagine you're in Florence. Imagine you're at Plato's Symposium where they're gathered around the table. This is not just me loving you and you loving me.

It's we loving She.

It's us loving the First Principles.

I can't speak the First Principles without your attention.

Your question, your attention, your investigation, and your wisdom are going to make it deeper and bigger. So, you're not an extra. This is not a question of whether or not I should do this for myself. No, **the world is hanging in the balance, literally**.

We're at this leading edge of culture where we have this responsibility to articulate these First Principles—and they should live long after our names are forgotten. This is for the sake of She. This is the Unique Self Symphony.

So with your permission, I want to just say it straight. *There's no extra on the set. Those of us here, we need to be here together.*

EVOLUTIONARY LOVE CODE: REALITY IS MOTIVATED BY PLEASURE

Reality is motivated by pleasure.

The highest pleasure is transformation.

Transformation equals evolution.

The highest pleasure of transformation is to know that your transformation transforms everything.

The highest transformation possible is to participate in the transformation of God.

The highest pleasure of evolution is to know that your evolution evolves everything.

And the highest evolution possible is to participate in the evolution of God.

In other words:

- Reality is motivated by pleasure.
- The highest pleasure is transformation.
- Transformation equals evolution.
- Reality is a series of transformations.

- And my transformation is only understandable in the context of this series of transformations.
- My transformation is the next stage in the transformation of Reality itself. I am the next transformation.

But it's deeper than that.

- Reality is motivated by pleasure.
- The highest pleasure is transformation.
- Transformation equals evolution.

Let's get that. There's pleasure in transformation.

Transformation is work.

- It takes effort.
- It takes commitment.
- It takes ecstasy.
- It takes rapture.
- It takes focus.
- It takes discipline.
- It takes sacrifice.

But all of that is part of pleasure.

We have a very narrow view of pleasure. Pleasure is more than ice cream, number one.

And number two, getting pleasure from ice cream is a great art, it's actually not so simple.

How do you get pleasure from ice cream?

How are you blown away by ice cream?

How does ice cream literally fuck you open until you're just dazzled by the goodness of Reality?

Getting pleasure from something I've already tasted before.

I'm no longer in the "counterfeit" pleasure of novelty—which is not counterfeit, it's not wrong. It just doesn't sustain.

Reality gives us an initial burst, an initial outbreak of pleasure, what's called by some of the mystics in the interior sciences "arousal from above." Arousal from above is the first steak.

No, I'm not going to say steak, because steaks are usually created through brutality to animals, so if you're doing steak you should be doing free range. **Being brutal to animals is one of the great tragedies of this century and we're going to look at it in fifty years and we're going to be completely shamed, so easy on the steak**. Don't eat a steak unless you know, minimally, that the animal wasn't tortured for three months for your steak. You don't want to be participating in that.

So instead, wow, the first time I tasted that ice cream or the first time I ate those gorgeous vegetables.

To get pleasure from your ice cream;

To get pleasure from physicality;

To get pleasure from the five senses;

To get pleasure from your mind;

To get pleasure from your body beyond the first time

Remember, was it twenty years ago, twenty-five years ago—oh my God, I'm so dating myself, this is so embarrassing—but how did Madonna sing it? *Like a virgin for the very first time.*

But she got it right, Madonna. Thank you, sister.

In the lineage traditions of the interior sciences, "like a virgin for the very first time" is the definition of enlightenment. Enlightenment means to revirginate.

To revirginate is the ability to be blown away just like the first time we did it.

When we love each other, we're blown away like it's for the first time.

TRANSFORMATION IS THE HIGHEST LEVEL OF PLEASURE

There are levels of pleasure. There is ice cream, that's level one, but there are lots of levels.

The highest level of pleasure is the pleasure of transforming.

There is the sacrifice, the commitment, the goodness, the love, the pain, the ecstasy, the joy, *but it's all pleasure*. There's a pleasure of transformation.

That pleasure literally animates subatomic particles. Subatomic particles are filled in their interior with pleasure. We can access it. It lives in you, because we are billions, trillions of quarks, hadrons, leptons, muons, then subatomic particles, atoms, molecules, macromolecules.

It all lives in us. And it's why we're driven by pleasure because Reality itself is driven by pleasure.

Pleasure drives Reality. Reality has what we might call desire. There's a desire in Reality that moves the whole story. It's the appetite of Cosmos. It's the allurement, to put it in evolutionary science terms—it's the electromagnetic field, it's the strong and the weak nuclear forces, it's the gravitational force. What's under gravity? Nothing. There's an allurement that drives the whole thing.

Love is the precise balance between allurement (I'm drawn towards) and autonomy (the independence of my trajectory). In the integrated, synergized balance between the two we get love, we get Eros.

Eros whose interior quality is pleasure. Eros drives Reality.

What is Eros?

- Eros is the experience of radical aliveness seeking, desiring ever deeper contact and ever larger wholeness.
- Eros drives subatomic particles, and it drives you and me. It's one Eros. That's what we mean.

It's not fanciful. It's not a declaration. It's one love. It's one heart. It's one Eros all the way up and all the way down.

This process of evolution, which is a series of transformations, awakens in me and then I transform.

And the same pleasure that drives the entire process is what moves the whole thing. Everything is moved by this balance of allurement and autonomy. And there's pleasure in both. It's called Eros. The interior quality of Eros is pleasure.

Pathological fragmentation, pathological division is painful, it's not pleasurable. It's the opposite of pleasure.

The highest pleasure is transformation.

- And the highest transformation is to know that your transformation literally transforms the whole thing.

THE GOD YOU DON'T BELIEVE IN DOESN'T EXIST

The god you don't believe in doesn't exist.

The small god, the caricatured god, the god who says, "I love this nation, I hate this nation," the Aztec and Mayan god who says, "Let's rip out 10,000 virgins' hearts," or the strain of god that says, "Let's kill all the men, women, and children."

No. The god you don't believe in doesn't exist. It's a social construction of a distortion of Reality that happens as consciousness evolves until it clarifies.

Consciousness is a series of transformations.

Just like exteriors are a series of transformations—subatomic particles until hominids until us, a series of transformations—**interiors are a series of transformations in our worldview.** The trajectory is the evolution of culture and consciousness, which itself is the evolution of Eros. It's the evolution of love.

When you bring that all together, you realize the god you don't believe in doesn't exist.

God is the Reality of the whole thing. God is both the personal that holds us and the quality of personhood that lives in me and lives in you. That quality of personhood is part of the larger Field of Personhood.

It's one of the great mistakes of the meditative traditions that they emphasized only the impersonal and not the personal. They actually dance together; Reality is a dialectic of personal and impersonal.

The quality of personhood that lives between us is the personhood that drives the Cosmos that lives in me. God is the Reality of the whole thing, personhood and impersonal:

- All of the laws of physics.
- All of the laws of chemistry.
- All of infotech; all of biotech.
- All of culture and every stage of history from matter to life to mind.

All of that is God.

When I transform, when I evolve, as the leading edge of transformation I am evolving God.

You've got to get it in your body; you have to enter the inside of the inside.

The mind can barely even begin to wrap around it. You've got to expand into an open, free consciousness, an open, free space so you can actually begin to imagine:

- My evolution is the evolution of God, literally.
- My transformation is the transformation of God.

God says, "I can't transform without you." "I love you so much," says the Infinite quality of Cosmos, "that I can't do it without you. So I'm waiting for you. Let's hold hands. Let's transform together."

That's what it means to be madly in love. Wow!

CHAPTER THREE

FIRST PRINCIPLES & FIRST VALUES: THE URGENT & ECSTATIC MORAL IMPERATIVE OF OUR TIME

Episode 206 — September 20, 2020

EVOLUTION FROM SEPARATE SELF THROUGH TRUE SELF TO UNIQUE SELF

In the mid-1990s, there was an explosion of channeling. All channeling means is *you get a clear inner voice that speaks*. One of the expressions of that was this movement from what they called back then, the "third density" to "fourth density." All third density means is the separate self; in our language, we call that the separate self.

It's the separate self who is in a win/lose metrics success story, where everything is about *I*:

- Am I getting my needs met?
- Am I being taken care of?
- Do I have control?
- Do I look good?

That is the win/lose metrics success story: *Do I have enough? What's my status? What do I look like?* Living in that story seems like, *Well, I guess maybe you could use*

some therapy, but it's not such a big deal. What's the problem? Everybody lives in that story.

That story is the source of fundamental existential risk: the risk to our very existence and the catastrophic risks. The risks that cause enormous suffering, like a pandemic, are all rooted in us living within that win/lose metrics success story.

SUCCESS SUMMIT: SUCCESS 1.0, SUCCESS 2.0, SUCCESS 3.0

About five or six years ago, I was privileged to host a summit to which I invited my colleague and dear friend John Mackey, the chair of Whole Foods and who at the time was serving as chairman of the Center for Integral Wisdom. There were about sixty or seventy other teachers from around the world—Ben Jealous, who later ran for governor in Maryland, Jack Canfield, a woman named Lynne Twist, who works in the finance field, my dear friend Michael Bernard Beckwith, Warren Farrell, and Adam Bellow. Tony Hsieh from Zappos came. Shep Gordon was there. It was an incredible cast of characters.

The entire topic of this success summit, which we called Success 3.0, was to look at the levels of success. I want to use this to set our intention today.

- The first stage, Success 1.0, means, *I'm successful because I was obedient to God's will.* It's a form of premodern success.

And it's quite beautiful. When the great religions expressed God's will, it was gorgeous and fantastic, but it was also, of course, quite limited because the great religions often expressed God's will in distorted ways. They projected corrupt or distorted human will onto the divine. That happened throughout the history of the churches. It's one of the great tragedies of premodernity.

Success 1.0 means *I'm obedient to God. I'm successful because I was successful in my obedience.*

Then along comes Success 2.0, and it's no longer about being obedient to God. It's the modern notion of success:

- I'm successful because I have accumulated goods. I've sold them at a profit, and therefore I've been successful.
- I've exerted effort.
- I've shown up for work.
- I've created commodities. I've exchanged them.
- I've gained a skill and sold that skill in the market.

There are all sorts of other values at play in modernity, but ultimately the experience of success is: *I am in a contemporary success story that's governed by win/lose metrics. I'm a separate self. I'm competing against everyone else. The universe is a mechanistic universe. I'm a cog in that universe. I need to stand out and be successful* (again, governed by win/lose metrics).

So it means that within every company, team, government agency, and within every department of every agency, there's always competition—there's always win/lose metrics. *I'm governed by whether I'm successful: that's success 2.0.*

The entire point of this success summit was to say: *That's a disaster. Success 2.0 will destroy society.* For example, there were thousands of people who were aware that a pandemic was coming—in various agencies in government—but no one was going to whistle-blow it to the public because no one wanted to lose their status in the hierarchy of success. Wow! That's a shocking reality. It's all about the success of the individual person, so we were not warned about the pandemic. For example, limited supplies of masks were largely due to win/lose contracts for companies who make masks.

The entire movement that created the bioterrorism initiatives—which was related to the testing of the Covid-19 virus, patented by the United States and developed under strange circumstances, to say the least—it was all based on win/lose metrics between countries.

And the Chinese Communist Party not sharing information was based on a win/lose metrics too.

We've got to move out of that; that's third-density, separate self reality.

Fourth density, in this image—and I'm just using this as an image—is the move from separate self to True Self: *I'm one with the entire Field of Consciousness, and Consciousness lives underneath and breathes Reality into existence.*

Based on the best philosophical and physical information we have available, based on all streams of data, that's our best understanding of Reality.

Consciousness underlies everything and breathes Reality into existence, and I'm inseparable from the Field of Consciousness. That's the beginning of fourth-density reality.

But then I realize I'm not just separate, and I'm not just one with the Field of Consciousness. I moved from separate self to True Self—so what's the third?

Unique Self:

- ◆ I'm not separate from the larger Field.
- ◆ I'm one with the larger Field.
- ◆ But I'm also not absorbed in the larger Field.
- ◆ *I'm a unique expression of the larger Field.*
- ◆ I'm an irreducibly unique, individuated expression of that larger Field.
- ◆ I'm literally Reality having a *me* experience.

I'm part of the Field, in devotion to the Field. I'm the paradoxical expression of sameness: I'm the same, I'm one with, and yet I'm distinct from, I'm separate. What's the resolution of that? Uniqueness.

It's a gorgeous idea. It's huge. It took me twenty years to understand clearly that separateness and uniqueness are actually not the same thing.

EVOLUTIONARY UNIQUE SELF: I AM A UNIQUE CONFIGURATION OF THE EVOLUTIONARY LOVE THAT ANIMATES ALL OF COSMOS

Then I deepen my density, as it were, from living in a consciousness of Unique Self, to realizing that I'm not just a Unique Self. *I'm a Unique Self living in an evolutionary context.* **I have an evolutionary relationship to life; the entire pulse of evolution lives awake and alive in me, so I'm Evolutionary Unique Self.**

I move from *Homo sapiens* to *Homo amor*. *Homo amor* means *I'm a hero*. The hero is the early adopter of *Homo amor*. **Homo amor means I'm living a different quality of consciousness. It means I have absorbed everything that's come through me.**

Everything that's come before lives in me. Plant consciousness lives in me. Animal consciousness lives in me. There's much more continuity between animals and human beings than we once thought. There's enormous continuity but there's also discontinuity. There's a momentous leap forward in human consciousness.

But human consciousness has to embrace all of animal consciousness. And the animal means the feeling of self-evident goodness when we touch each other's hearts, when we touch each other's bodies, and when we touch each other existentially and intellectually. All of that lives in me.

- I'm Evolutionary Unique Self.
- I have my unique distinctions.
- I'm one with the larger Field of Consciousness.

I experience the inside of the larger Field of Consciousness as exploded with love. I know that love is absolutely real, not a social construction. It is that which governs all of Reality. And I'm a unique configuration of the evolutionary love that animates all of Cosmos.

THE CRISIS IN REALITY TODAY IS A CRISIS OF FIRST PRINCIPLES AND FIRST VALUES

Let's talk for a second about First Principles, just so we get where we're going this year. The collapse of Reality today, at its core, is based on a collapse of narrative. **There's a failure of Story.** Story is not a conjecture. When we say story or narrative, we mean the best integration—at any time in history—of ordinating, guiding values and guiding principles. Let's feel that.

At particular points in Reality, we gather together the best wisdom on the planet. Earlier, in premodernity, for example, First Principles or First Values didn't exist. Every religion claimed it had its own First Principles and Values, and no one else's was right. So there was a hijacking of this notion of First Principles and Values.

When we realize that the crisis in Reality today is a crisis of First Principles and First Values, we're saying something beyond important. **If we understand that the breakdown comes from a *failure* of First Principles, we understand that the breakthrough comes from the restoration, as well as the evolution, the articulation, of a *new* set of First Principles and First Values.**

That's what we mean by a new Story. A new Story means a new set of First Principles and First Values that integrate the best of premodern, modern, and postmodern wisdom, woven together into a larger story, a larger narrative that accounts for more facts, for more data, for more interior science and more exterior science than any other possibility. That's our best knowledge of Reality today.

Now, included in that knowing is the unknowing. The cloud of unknowing always hovers above First Principles. We always stand reverential and in devotion at the edge of the mystery. First Principles don't pretend to dispel all the uncertainty. What we do is we claim our certainties. There are First Values and First Principles that drive Cosmos, and they've collapsed. We have no relationship with them. So we need to find that again.

POISED BETWEEN UTOPIA AND DYSTOPIA, THE WAY FORWARD IS TO ARTICULATE A NEW STORY BASED ON FIRST PRINCIPLES AND FIRST VALUES

There is today a crisis of intimacy, which is at the core of the global action paralysis and the global action confusion. This is at the core of existential risk, the potential second shock of existence that threatens our planet.

1. The first shock of existence was the realization at the dawn of civilization that individual human beings would die—the death of the human being.
2. The second shock of existence is the realization that we've brought ourselves to the brink of the death of humanity.

It's a Renaissance moment, meaning we can have an enormous Renaissance—we're poised between utopia and dystopia—**or we can break down ultimately and finally**. We're in another da Vinci moment.

- We're in this time between worlds and time between stories in which the way forward is to articulate a new Story based on First Principles and First Values.

That is the most urgent moral imperative of this moment in time.

FIRST PRINCIPLES AND FIRST VALUES INTEGRATE PREMODERN, MODERN, AND POSTMODERN INSIGHTS

First Principles and First Values include the best premodern wisdom. For example, today I'm not shaven. I'm not shaven because part of the premodern tradition that I was sourced in is a Hebrew wisdom tradition. And today is the second day of Rosh Hashanah, so I'm not shaving today because for two days, that's the practice. We'll talk a little bit about *shofar* (a shamanic instrument made of a ram's horn), which comes from a premodern context. Barbara will talk about the planetary Pentecost today, which is an integration of a premodern idea of Pentecost.

- The religions have an enormously important voice, and we can cull and extrapolate from the religions the best of First Principles and First Values.
- Then we go to modernity, and we identify the best First Principles and First Values in modernity.
- Then we go to postmodernity, and we identify the best First Principles and First Values in postmodernity.

Then we weave them all together.

That's the da Vinci move in this generation. It's the most subtle and powerful move, and it's the only move that will avoid inevitable suffering of a magnitude that's unimaginable—and ultimately, the potential and probable death of humanity.

This is a moment in which we have to resonate into and articulate First Principles and First Values, which means we have to claim certainties— tentative, humble, but audacious certainties.

- What are the ordinating values of Cosmos?
- What does it mean to ontologize love, meaning to know that love is real and that it moves all the way up and all the way down?
- What's our narrative of identity?
- What's our narrative of value?
- What's our narrative of power?
- What's our narrative of desire?
- What's our sexual narrative?
- What's our narrative of community?
- What's our narrative of relationship?

It's not *all a social construction of Reality*. It's not—as my friend and colleague Yuval Harari would say—*a fiction*. For example, in his book *Sapiens*,

Harari talks about Gaddafi's notions of human rights and universal human rights as *equal fictions, social constructions of Reality*. No, that's a source of collapse. Blessings to Yuval. We haven't met. I say *my friend* because he's a colleague. He's a good man, but he's making tragic mistakes that are undermining the core fabric of Reality.

We have to articulate a new set of First Principles and First Values. That is the revolution: that articulation, that deployment, and that downloading into the source code of culture.

WE NEED TO REWEAVE THE INFORMATION ECOLOGY TO ARTICULATE AN EVOLVING SET OF FIRST PRINCIPLES AND FIRST VALUES

We have to become a new information ecology and look at the news every day through the prism of how it relates to First Principles and First Values. That's what we want to do. We want to become a new source of wisdom and information. We have to reweave the information ecology, and we have to literally re-soul Reality with an evolving set of First Principles and First Values. It's an evolving set. It's not that we're merely going to reclaim old premodern First Principles and First Values and just put them back at the center. That's what the perennial philosophy did, which was a mistake. No, it's an *evolving* set of First Principles and First Values.

And the revolution of First Principles is at the very core of everything.

- ◆ First Principles are ancient, time-honored, and venerable, even as they are evolutionary, emergent, and new.
- ◆ First Principles weave together the most crucial validated truths from all the wisdom streams—premodern, modern, and postmodern—into a new whole, greater than the sum of their parts.
- ◆ First Principles are what we have referred to as the new Story, a new *Dharma*, or a global ethos for a global civilization.

- First Principles inform the core narratives of society. Those include the core Universe Story, as well as all the derivative narratives of identity, communion, power, value, and desire.
- First Principles articulate an evolving universal grammar of value.
- First Principles are implicitly shared by all the many paths.

This is the revolution.

PRAYER: I WANT TO KNOW WHAT LOVE IS

Who's up for praying? Are we ready to pray? We've got a new text of prayer, a text that we began with. Let's pray together.

I want to know what love is. That's a prayer. Let's pray it like we never have before on this first day of Rosh Hashanah, as we're ready to move into Ramadan, the great Islamic holiday. Let's pray. *I want to know what love is.*

One communion: every atheist, every Jew, every Chinese Taoist, every secularist, every agnostic, every Islamicist, every Christian of every kind, everyone all over the world, we're one communion, and we're asking, all of us, one question.

We're asking: *I want to know what love is; I ask you to show me.*

THE FIRST VALUE OF COSMOS: LOVE IS REAL

Love is a feeling inside. That's a First Principle and First Value, but here's how it works. **It's not just a subjective feeling inside me.**

- **Love is the inside of Reality itself.**

The best integration of all the data is that Reality is animated by Eros, by allurement. What's underneath gravity? Nothing. Gravity is allurement. Electromagnetism is allurement. It's the precise balance between the vector of individuation and autonomy—*I'm free,* and *I'm me*—and allurement—*I'm allured to you, drawn to you, and lonely without you.* That movement is fundamental to all levels of Cosmos.

That's what it means to ontologize love.

***Love is Real* is a First Value of Cosmos.**

That movement doesn't begin with the human being. Love is not mere human sentiment. It's not ordinary. Love is the most extraordinary force. The Cosmos doesn't stop at carbon. It keeps going. It doesn't stop at macromolecules.

It keeps going because love is creative.

Love evolves. Love's not just eternal. Love evolves. So love gets more and more divine. There's more love to come. There's more God to come. Love evolves. **The evolution of love is a First Principle.**

♦ **First Value: Love is Real. First Principle: Love evolves.**

And it evolves all the way up and down, and takes us all the way home. Love is a feeling inside, but it means *its insides are lined with love.* In the original text: *tocho ratzuf ahavah.*

The interior face of the Cosmos is lined with love, and every exterior is the allurement between hadrons, muons, leptons, protons, and electrons—the atoms held together. The rock is held together by sentient, living atoms and molecules, all the way up and all the way down.

Love becomes awake, love evolves until it awakens uniquely as me and you, and I realize my love story, your love story, is chapter and verse in the Universe: A Love Story. Wow!

THE NEW EMERGENCE: UNIQUE SELF SYMPHONY

Feel the beauty of this moment. Feel also what's happening. There is an emergence of a new level of intimacy, a new level of collective consciousness, a New Human, and a New Humanity, *Homo amor*. We call this a Unique Self Symphony.

In the Unique Self Symphony, every person is part of the larger field— *True Self*—as well as a unique expression of the field: *Unique Self*. Everyone is an evolutionary expression; *I am evolution: Evolutionary Unique Self*, each playing our unique instruments. And then we come together as a revolutionary force from the bottom up, a mighty, roaring river, a river of *God as us*, even as we're held by Cosmos, in which we each play our unique instrument.

From that diversity, as we listen to each other, what emerges is a new score, music, and vision. What emerges is the symphony of *Homo amor* in which every instrument is utterly necessary.

That's the next step. That's the bottom-up Self-Organizing Universe.

Oh my God, that's Unique Self Symphony.

CHAPTER FOUR

EVOLVING THE SOURCE CODE OF CONSCIOUSNESS AND CULTURE

First Values and First Principles 01 —
October 3, 2020

THE MOST URGENT MORAL IMPERATIVE OF OUR TIME IS THE ARTICULATION OF FIRST PRINCIPLES AND FIRST VALUES

Welcome to this first short conversation introducing First Principles and First Values, fixing our broken information ecology and evolving the source code of consciousness and culture at this time between worlds and a time between stories.

We want to begin to understand what we mean by First Principles and First Values and why we believe they are the most urgent moral imperative of our time.

They are our great joy and our most urgent responsibility.

Let's try and name the moment of time that we're in. We call this a da Vinci moment. It's a Renaissance moment which had recently been struck by the Black Death in Europe—and the Black Death in Europe was, according to many accounts, an actual act of biological warfare. At the siege of Caffa, the Tatars, the Mongolian attackers, were devastated by plague and according to several eyewitness accounts they actually hurled plague-infested corpses into Caffa by catapult. So it was actually an act of biological warfare of desperate bioterrorism, if you will, as an act of war.

We, of course, know that the pandemic today is unclear in its source, and it looks fairly certain that it had something to do with gain-of-function research, that is to say research carried on in the Wuhan laboratory, coordinated by both the United States and China.

And **apparently something went wrong**. We're not sure who or what made it go wrong. It looks like it was on the Chinese side. We're not sure if it was intentional or unintentional, but we know that there is a real possibility that the pandemic was an act of biological warfare.

- Certainly a genuine possibility.
- It reaches to a probability when you gather all the facts that it was created by human beings and aimed at human beings.

That's a big deal, but that's just a surface analogy with the Renaissance.

The Renaissance was also a moment in which the old story doesn't work:

- The Black Death sweeps Europe.
- The old rules clearly don't apply.
- The old principles don't hold us.
- Reality is literally coming apart at the seams.

And it was impossible for da Vinci and his cohort to enter every village in Europe to heal the plague.

And trade and business and science were all coming together and creating new possibilities—

- New ways of looking at what a human being is in his or her very core.
- New ways of looking at what communion and community might mean.

- New ways of looking at Divinity and the Infinite.
- New ways of looking at how business should be conducted.
- New ways of looking at how knowledge is gathered.
- New ways of understanding love.
- New ways of understanding trust.

It's a new universe story based on new information, a new narrative of identity, new narratives of power, new narratives of desire. Everything was changing.

These changes in the Renaissance did not occur in the broad population; there were only about a thousand people total involved in the Renaissance, mostly around Florence and some other cities in Italy. They got together and realized:

We need to retell the story. We need a new Story. That new Story has to be based on a new understanding of First Values and First Principles of Cosmos.

They tried to extrapolate the best universal principles from premodernity— the time period up until the Renaissance—and then move forward, evolve, and re-understand God and man and woman and the human body and medicine and the scientific method and gnosis and desire and power and community and identity.

It was this revisioning that birthed modernity.

THE DIGNITIES AND DISASTERS OF MODERNITY

To the precise extent that this revisioning was smart and deep and profound, sharp, penetrating, accurate, and aligned with the nature of Cosmos, it brought great blessings, the great dignities of modernity. To the precise extent that the story was flawed in its sciences and its humanities, to the precise extent that it misunderstood:

- The faults in the plotline

- ◆ The misunderstanding of the nature of matter
- ◆ The misunderstanding of the nature of the human being as a separate self
- ◆ Matter as inert, the atom as the basic separate unit of Reality—those were mistakes.

The disasters of modernity were born. There were great limitations.

But they described something that had deep truth, and it gave great blessing. Understanding the human being as an individual as an individuated separate self rendered the human as a dignified being, independent of the church and independent of the feudal lord.

Understanding matter as individual units allowed for the move from classification to measurement, and the measurement of motion and of particles and birthed modern science with many of its important and wondrous achievements and blessings. It ultimately birthed the Industrial Revolution and then the Information Revolution. These are some of the dignities of modernity.

At the same time:

- ◆ The misunderstanding of the human being.
- ◆ The failures in the plotline of the story.
- ◆ The failures in understanding a larger Field of Value.
- ◆ The failures in understanding human identity in its depth as part of the larger field and as a unique expression of the larger field.
- ◆ The foundational structural mistakes.

All of these misdirections in the plotline of the story ultimately yielded what would become the disasters of modernity.

The disasters of modernity birthed all of the forms of alienation, all of the forms of what we would call the global intimacy disorder, ultimately emerging in the late twentieth century.

The world became a vast, complicated system with no inherent allurement between the parts:

- Based on a win/lose metrics success story,
- A success story governed by win-lose metrics all the way up and all the way down the system,
- In which human beings competed,
- In which human beings had no innate value,
- In which our universe story collapsed into a dogmatic, reductionist, materialist story.

All of the tragedies in the story yielded all of the existential risks that we face today.

We face today a set of existential risks, a set of challenges to our very existence, that have never been faced by humanity before.

Our very future is at stake. The challenge at this moment of time is what we have referred to as the second shock of existence.

THE FIRST AND SECOND SHOCKS OF EXISTENCE EVOKE NEW GNOSIS

The first shock of existence at the dawn of human history was the realization of death—that the skull grins in at the banquet—the realization that the human being has a finite period of time, after which we die.

Now, we know death to be a night between two days—there is a continuity of consciousness. Nonetheless, the experience of death, the radical finiteness of our existence on this Earth creates a context which demands our response, which demands that we choose with great depth, because every choice is a genuine option. It demands that we discern with all

75

our powers of concentration and focus and wisdom and intention and contemplation and meditation and prayer and searching to understand the nature of Reality.

The realization of the first shock of existence birthed a new gnosis, a new knowing, which unfolded as all of the great moments in human culture and in human history and in human flourishing.

This realization, this encounter with the death of the human being birthed all of civilization.

We went through all these stages of civilization until we came to the moment we're in now, where the fault lines in the story of modernity, all of its disasters, have brought us to this moment in time where we face not only the first but the second shock of existence.

The second shock of existence is the realization not of the inevitable death of the individual human being but of the potential death of humanity. The death of humanity means the loss of all future. It's a shocking realization: there will be no future.

All the human flourishing of the future will disappear, and the present will either fall into a dystopian vision in which human potential and human flourishing will be radically undercut as the systems of civilization break down, or the dystopian manifestation will ultimately lead to an extinction event.

Those are very viable possibilities for seven or eight different reasons:

- Nuclear weapons that are on high alert with only ten-minute warning sequences to prevent false alarms.
- Climate change leading to ecosystem collapse and extinction-level events in which the entire system upon which everything depends just breaks down, and then all the second systems break down afterwards.

76

- Pandemics that we now actually see can stop Reality—and this is an extremely minor pandemic that we're in the middle of right now in 2020.
- Artificial intelligence and a number of dystopian scenarios that are real, according to the best researchers in the field.
- Non-state actors with access to advanced technologies that have exponential destructive potential. These technologies are available in a far more democratized way, whether it's CRISPR genome technology or bioterrorism technology, etc.
- There are three or four other scenarios.

These are all fundamental existential risks. To deal with them all, and to deal with their implications, we need to create a new Story.

WIN/LOSE SUCCESS STORY LEADS TO DYSTOPIAN SCENARIOS

The old story doesn't work. The success story based on win/lose metrics in which everyone is in competition with everyone else:

- Every city
- Every nation
- Every department in every government
- Every person
- Every family
- Every sports team
- Every region
- Every company
- Every division within every company

This success story governed by win/lose metrics is what generated this Reality, this vast complicated system, which is fragile, which breaks down easily, where the energy grid can be easily destroyed, where supply lines break down.

This entire structure is not tenable. It's not resilient. It can't make it. What we need to do in order to address the many existential risks is to create global coherence.

None of these issues can be addressed locally. **And because of win/lose metrics, no single nation can it take upon themselves, because there is not enough gain.** All of humanity will benefit, not just one nation. It requires an enormous outlaying of resources.

The story in which humanity now lives is one in which no one will take responsibility.

For example, no one will stop the AI race even though there's a genuine recognition of its potential existential risk to the entire system, because everyone realizes that if they stop, someone else is going to continue, and then it will be bad actors who won the AI race, which will then allow totalitarian possibility, so we have to stay in, etc.

Because of win/lose metrics within the context of a vast, fragile, complicated system prone to breakdown, we've actually undercut all the antifragile systems that would allow for resistance. **Those two factors are the source of these dystopian scenarios facing us:**

1. The failed narrative of identity, the failed story, the success story governed by win/lose metrics.
2. The vast complicated system in which there's no inherent allurement.

We need to move beyond them, to transform them, in order to access a utopia which is literally right there—it's just about available; we have capacities that we've never had.

We have the power of the ancient gods.

We have capacities, through nanotech and biotech, beyond imagination, infotech brought together with nanotech and biotech, possibilities for health, possibilities for wisdom—but we've abandoned the wisdom part.

We have focused on exterior technologies, but our interior technologies have broken down.

+ There's a breakdown of value.
+ There's a breakdown of a sense of there being a coherent story, so there's no allurement between the parts.

All that's left are separate parts and win/lose competition.

AT THIS PHASE SHIFT IN HUMAN HISTORY, WE MUST START THE RECONSTRUCTION PROJECT OF VALUE

The only way to move through this is to make the da Vinci move.

We're in the Renaissance.

+ It's a phase shift in human history.
+ It's a time between stories.
+ It's a time between worlds.

At that moment, da Vinci, Marsilio Ficino, and dozens of other figures came together—not more than a thousand at the core: funders, creators, articulators, deployers, disseminators, artists, creators of all kinds came together—**and articulated, based on intense study, and intense commitment a new vision of value, a new field of meaning.**

That new field became modernity.

Postmodernity then came and deconstructed that field, deconstructed the values of modernity and the claims of premodernity in a thousand different ways. Postmodernity made some important points and had some tragic flaws, but now it's time to move beyond postmodernity, beyond the deconstructive projects of modernity and its hyper-expression in postmodernity.

We now have to start the reconstructive project which has to articulate First Values and First Principles.

WE NEED A SET OF FIRST PRINCIPLES AND FIRST VALUES BEFORE WE CAN ARTICULATE A SHARED GLOBAL STORY

- You can't talk about AI without having a vision of what a Unique Self human being is. That's a First Principle of identity, the human being as a Unique Self, an innately valuable, irreducible expression of the Field of Consciousness.

- You can't talk about healing the global intimacy disorder without a vision based on the depth of science of what it means to live in an Intimate Universe.

- You can't have an understanding of evolution without understanding that evolution has direction—not direction as suggested by premodern dogmatic narratives, but direction as inherent in the clear knowing of science, which speak of the plotlines of evolution as moving towards more and more creativity, more and more uniqueness, more and more intimacy, more and more possible care and love and concern. **This is evolution as the evolution of love, Reality as the progressive deepening of intimacies.**

Without these First Values and First Principles, we can't even begin to articulate a set of policies, a shared global story that creates global coherence.

Without global coherence we can't move. When the Covid pandemic hit the world, no one got together to talk about it. There was no global meeting.

> *The pandemic knows no boundaries, and yet every individual country is trying to deal with it independently.*

In the United States, for example, every state is dealing with it independently. So you have a pandemic that knows no boundaries and you have a world that's filled with separate selves and separate countries competing according to boundaries and win/lose metrics. Wow! That's shocking.

The notion that the Chinese Communist Party has that *we can fight for the good of China against the rest of the world* fundamentally misunderstands the nature of Reality today.

Reality is global, and everything affects everything.

There is no local—there is only global.

But without a set of First Principles and First Values that allow us to address every single global challenge, every single existential risk, all of which are global problems, none of which are particularly local, **without a shared universal grammar of value, we probably won't make it through this time.**

If and when we do, **we must come together and articulate a universal grammar of value, non-dogmatic, evolving First Values and First Principles:**

- Based on the innate structure of Cosmos
- Based on an integration of the best validated knowledge from the great traditions of premodernity, the best validated knowledge of all the wisdom streams of modernity, and the leading validated insights of postmodernity

We weave them all together and what emerges is literally a new story, a new coming together of parts into a larger whole, a new configuration of intimacy.

It's only that new configuration of intimacy, that new story woven together by First Values and First Principles, as da Vinci and Ficino did in the Renaissance, that can actually take us through this perilous eleventh hour of humanity.

The single-most urgent moral imperative of the present and of the future—all generations of the future depend on it.

- There are potentially trillions of years left to human existence. We've just begun to manifest the wonder, the depth, the goodness, the truth, the beauty, the love that is Reality, Infinity becoming its most beautiful possibility. That's the possibility that stands before us.
- The alternative is that it ends in this generation or the next generation or the next 100 or 200 years.

Wow!

So let's do this. **Let's do this with a sense of joy, with a sense of trembling, with a sense of ecstatic urgency, with a sense of radical responsibility.**

We come together as this new Renaissance in this time between worlds, humbly; **humility has to infuse our every word.**

And yet we have to be audacious.

We have to swallow all of culture whole and then reorganize it, bring all these pieces of new information together and share this new Story, this global ethos for this global civilization.

Let's do it together.

Thank you.

CHAPTER FIVE

SURVEILLANCE CAPITALISM: "WE'RE GOING TO STEAL YOUR EXPERIENCE WITHOUT YOUR PERMISSION"

First Principles 02 — October 10, 2020

FIRST PRINCIPLES AND FIRST VALUES ACCOUNT FOR THE CRITIQUES OF NATURAL LAW AND PERENNIAL PHILOSOPHY

It is only by articulating a coherent and cogent vision of First Principles and First Values that we can navigate this eleventh hour of human existence, in which we stand poised between utopia and dystopia. **By First Principles and First Values, we mean the very structures of Cosmos that evolve over time, but in their root they apply across all time, they apply across all space, and they live innately in every human being.**

Now, for those of you who are philosophers, I'm of course aware that there were two major attempts to articulate what I'm calling First Principles and First Values. One of them was the "natural law" school of thought, and the related but distinct attempt by what are called the perennial philosophers. Both natural law and perennial philosophy have been in part correctly rejected by the postmodern academy.

When we say First Principles and First Values, we mean something which is way beyond the early conception of natural law. It also takes into account all the critiques of natural law, responds to them, and evolves our conception of what natural law might mean. Our notion of First Principles and First Values also takes into account all the criticisms of perennial philosophy, and evolves our vision of what perennial philosophy might become.

For those of you unfamiliar, perennial philosophy is a movement of early modernity that says that premodernity—where different religions and different systems were all arguing that they had the exclusive view of truth—**perennial philosophy said:** *Underneath all the surface structures of the different religions, there's a shared set of depth structures*. This shared set of depth structures was extrapolated from all the different traditions, gathered and articulated by the early perennial philosophers.

The problem with both perennial philosophy and natural law is that they claimed a lot to be natural or a depth structure of Cosmos, but was really a surface structure, influenced by particular historical epochs, influenced by particular ways of thinking, or rooted in particular social moments—but actually weren't really depth structures.

That's a big idea.

MISTAKEN ASSUMPTIONS OF NATURAL LAW AND PERENNIAL PHILOSOPHY

I'll just give you one example. There might have been, for example, a notion that particular kinds of sexuality are a violation of natural law, and that you should be burned at the stake, because "that's a violation of natural law." I'm giving an extreme example, but you get what I mean. That's actually not true, though. **That's not natural law. That particular vision of sexuality is actually a surface structure of Reality, not a depth structure**. That's an example of claiming something is a depth structure when it's really just a surface structure. That's an example of a mistake made in the name of natural law.

84

I'll give you an example from perennial philosophy. A classical mistake of the perennial philosophers is to say, "The only way to realize the full purpose of a human being is through a meditative path in which I nullify my sense of being distinct and I realize that I'm part of the great seamless coat of Cosmos, part of the Emptiness, part of the Field of One—I am True Self with all of Cosmos."

Now, that is true to some extent, but the perennial philosophers said that's the *only* way to come home, that's the only way to realize the purpose of human existence. So **they took one path and said that's the only path that can get you to the mountain—there is no other path.** As such, prayer was dismissed, and it disappeared. Embodiment was really not part of the conversation at all. There's a long list. The emergence of the feminine, the balance between the feminine and the masculine, the evolutionary impulse, the notion that the human being participates in evolution, the dialectic between being and becoming—all of that was left out by perennial philosophy.

CRITIQUES BY POSTMODERNITY OF NATURAL LAW AND PERENNIAL PHILOSOPHY

Postmodernity came to full fruition in the last thirty or forty years, but strains of it existed for the last 150 years. **Essentially, postmodernity critiqued and dismissed natural philosophy and perennial philosophy on multiple levels. These criticisms are true but partial.**

* Natural law made claims and said, "Oh, this is actually a depth structure," for example, a particular form of sexuality being forbidden, when that was really a surface structure. Based on those kinds of critiques, natural law was completely thrown out. It was basically said that natural law didn't take into account culture, that natural law fell into the "myth of the given," that natural law didn't understand all the influences that created our understandings of Reality—so natural law was dismissed.

85

- ◆ Perennial philosophy was thrown out for claiming one path as the only path, not realizing that it's many paths and one mountain.

Here's the key. **Postmodernism's favorite activity is to attack and kill perennial philosophy and to attack and kill natural law—because postmodernism has a hidden agenda.**

- ◆ Postmodernism says there is no shared narrative.
- ◆ Postmodernism says there are no universals.
- ◆ Postmodernism is a scathing attack on any form of universals and any form of a shared story of humanity.

And it has good reason for this, and bad reason.

The good reason is that postmodernism is traumatized by premodern saying, *We've got the grand narrative and we're going to oppress everyone else who's not in our grand narrative.* Modernity had its own version of a grand narrative and anyone who is out of modernity's grand narrative gets oppressed. So postmodernity says, *No, these grand narratives are all wrong. Anyone trying to do a grand narrative is really hiding their drive for power. So we need to expose the true power motive and deconstruct all the grand narratives.*

That's called the great deconstruction of postmodernity.

POSTMODERNITY'S CRITIQUE OF PERENNIALISM AND NATURAL LAW IS TRUE BUT PARTIAL, AND IT IGNORES RESPONSIBILITY TO ANY LARGER GRAND NARRATIVE—EXCEPT THE SUCCESS STORY

Foucault was an essential figure in this great deconstruction, but somewhere about halfway through his deconstruction he realized, *Wow, I'm deconstructing all grand narratives. I'm saying that there are no universals, there are no grand narratives.* Then he realizes, *But that itself is a universal. That itself is a grand narrative. I have a new grand narrative—there are no grand narratives. I have a new universal—there are no universals.*

86

Foucault realized that was a performative contradiction: postmodernity was being radically arrogant and saying "there are no universals" but claiming that as a universal.

In fact, that was the beginning of an opening of this very deep realization that natural law overreached and claimed surface structures as depth structures—for example, "this kind of sexuality is proscribed." I keep saying the example again so it's just very easy to follow. It was also the realization that perennialism had overreached by saying, "This is the only path, the perennial philosophy," when there are many gorgeous and sacred paths that can bring you home and into the realization of our true nature and the true nature of Reality.

However, **both perennialism and natural law were doing something very important. This is what postmodernity ignores**.

There's a second reason for postmodernity's attack: it doesn't want to be responsible to any larger grand narrative.

- Postmodernity wants to be free.
- Postmodernity in this sense is a hyper-expression of modernity itself.
- Postmodernity wants to be free to be involved in this mad drive for material accumulation, for success.

The only narrative of the human being that does live in modernity/postmodernity is what we've called the "success story": a rivalrous story governed by win/lose metrics where the only goal is accumulation.

THE NERVOUS SYSTEM OF THE PLANET IS THE WEB, THE WORLDWIDE VIRTUAL WORLD

Now, you might think that's a little bit of an exaggeration. You might think I'm taking that too far. So I want to invite you to a particular book called *The Age of Surveillance Capitalism* by Shoshana Zuboff. It's actually a great work. It's not an easy read, but it's about the inner structure of the nervous system of the planet today.

The nervous system of the planet is the web, is the worldwide virtual world.

Now, everyone who's listening now I assume has used Google, Facebook perhaps, Amazon, WhatsApp, and multiple other applications all over the web. These are all normal applications that we use. What we're unaware of is—as Zuboff points out very intensely, tracking original documents from the year 2000 until today—**what Google is really doing**. What happens is you do a Google search, but when you do a Google search what you search, how you searched, how you put in the query, all that information is captured.

In fact, Google has created a crawling of the web over an unimaginable number of websites around the world. **Every time you put information into the web:**

- Let's say you use Gmail—**Google is reading your mail and drawing information from your mail.**
- How long did your mouse hover before you clicked on a link?
- How quickly did you make a decision?
- Every time you send a picture.
- Every time you send a text:
  - How many question marks did you use?
  - How did you use spacing?
  - Did you make mistakes?

What's actually happening is that your entire set of preferences—implied from what you did, not what you said—**your personality, your emotions, everything you write... nothing disappears. It's all being fed into an extremely complex beyond imagination artificial intelligence system**

driven by machine intelligence in order to build a profile of you. Then you are able to be manipulated through predictive analysis in order to either sell you something or control you in a particular way.

GOOGLE'S BUSINESS MODEL IS SURVEILLANCE CAPITALISM

For example, Google's business model is not about organizing the world's information, which is what Google began with. It was a public presentation. But in the early 2000s dot-com explosion, the bubble burst, and Google was pressured by venture capital funds that had invested in Silicon Valley. **Google then gradually shifted its operation and essentially became a surveillance capitalist**—a term coined by Zuboff—**which means *you're being surveilled all the time, for profit.***

Information about you is poured into a machine intelligence-driven exponential AI supercomputer of the kind that's able to infer—from every jot and tittle that you write—your mood, your interior states, your preferences. An entire personality profile is then built around you and you start receiving highly targeted ads.

FACEBOOK HIJACKS YOUR ATTENTION, TAKES YOUR INFORMATION, AND TARGETS YOU WITH ADS, THEREBY COMPROMISING THE FREE MOVEMENT OF ECONOMY AND GOVERNANCE

Everything you put into Gmail or Facebook is read and registered. This is not Facebook "creating a platform to interconnect the world." That's not Facebook's business model. That's a lie. **Facebook's business model is taking all the information, all of your hijacked attention, downloading it into an artificial intelligence system, and then targeting you with ads.**

Those ads can be economic, but those ads can also be about health, and those ads can also be about how you vote.

All of democracy is built on the voter and the consumer. The free movement of economy and the free movement of governance is the innovation of democracy.

WE ARE UNAWARE OF THE THREAT TO UNIVERSAL HUMAN RIGHTS

Homo sapiens first appeared about 100,000 years ago, and really only in the last several hundred years have we finally got to this huge innovation, this great evolution of consciousness—this great evolution of love called "universal human rights."

Universal human rights means that your will is sacrosanct, that you have the ability to collate information and make free decisions, that you own your future, that your will has sacred integrity, that you're an irreducibly unique person with irreducibly unique value.

These First Principles and First Values are completely ignored by Google, Facebook, WhatsApp, Verizon, Microsoft, and Amazon. **The entire tech plex basically assumes that your experience, your interiority, your interior experience is raw material to be stolen and subject to analysis, out of which emerges highly predictive analysis and then sold to advertisers**—corporations, political parties, etc.—**to manipulate you, move you to buy or vote in a particular direction.** However, you are unaware that all of that's happening.

That's what's so unique.

Imagine that you're Kasparov playing chess in the famous Deep Blue match, and artificial intelligence wipes you out. But the artificial intelligence that beat Kasparov thirty years ago is now completely outdated. Google's AlphaZero recently played Stockfish, which represented that old artificial intelligence, and essentially decimated the old artificial intelligence. There's this new level of machine-learning-driven artificial intelligence that's exponentially more advanced than what beat the greatest reigning chess grandmaster thirty years ago.

But all of that is hidden from you, used against your ability to make a free decision.

- What happens to your integrity as a voter? It becomes a joke.
- What happens to your integrity as a consumer? It becomes a joke.
- What happens to a free economy and free markets? It becomes a joke.
- What happens to a free democracy? It becomes a joke.

Are you beginning to get that?

THE FAILURE TO ARTICULATE THE CASE AGAINST THE TECH PLEX IS ROOTED IN A FAILURE OF FIRST PRINCIPLES AND FIRST VALUES

Someone mentioned just now in the chat box, "this is in *The Social Dilemma*." *The Social Dilemma* is quite a good documentary, and the person who made it met with some people at the Center, one particular person, over the last year and had some great conversations. *The Social Dilemma* focuses on social media with a small conversation around the larger issues.

The Social Dilemma, which is a great documentary, shares the same problem that Zuboff's book shares. The problem is that *The Social Dilemma* points out that **social media**—which is not exactly what I was focused on now—is **hijacking your attention**, and says correctly, "that's terrible."

But they're not sure why. They don't quite tell you why it's terrible that they're hijacking your attention. Aren't they just being like normal advertisers? *The Social Dilemma* movie can't quite answer that, so it says the reason it's terrible is *because it creates polarization: you get into a particular bubble of information and you keep seeing your own political views reinforced and exaggerated, so it creates great polarization.* **That is in part true, but that's not the core.**

Both *The Social Dilemma* and Zuboff's book miss the core of the whole thing. They're struggling to get it. They want to get it. They're on the edge but they can't quite articulate it.

By the way, Shoshana Zuboff, the author of *Surveillance Capitalism*, appears in the documentary *The Social Dilemma* and she also struggles to articulate it. Tristan Harris, the gentleman who made *The Social Dilemma* with a bunch of other people, is struggling to articulate—they can't quite get there. **The reason they can't get there is because there's a fundamental failure of First Values and First Principles.**

Shoshana Zuboff is outraged that this is happening but can't quite understand why it's so wrong because she refuses to articulate any sense of an evolving perennialism—not the old perennialism but an *evolving* perennialism, an evolving natural law, or what we might call shared First Values and First Principles. She understands that there's this big violation here, but cannot say what it's in violation of. So you read the book, and you get the outrage, you get what's happening, **but you're not quite sure why it matters**.

The same thing with *The Social Dilemma*, there's this outrage: *they're stealing my attention*. But big deal. Advertisers always steal our attention, that's what it's about. Why is that new? **Unfortunately, there's no understanding of First Principles and First Values.**

First Principles and First Values means:

- My interior experience is irreducibly unique.
- Feeling that experience is my source of wisdom.
- My attention and my unique quality of attention is my irreducible quality of the sacred.

- It's my attention that blooms Reality, it's my attention that's creative.

Under Surveillance Capitalism, under the tech plex, my ability to access my deepest quality of feeling Reality is blocked.

No one has a right to access my interior experience and then sell it to someone who's not me without my permission whose interests aren't aligned with mine.

However, you can't understand this violation without a deep articulation of Unique Self, which is one of the First Principles and First Values of Reality.

Without First Principles and First Values, you can't move.

SURVEILLANCE CAPITALISM: WE'RE GOING TO STEAL YOUR EXPERIENCE WITHOUT YOUR PERMISSION

I'm now going to read you six declarations of Google, which are now no longer published by Google, but were found by Zuboff in an early set of Google documents. Despite Google's current capturing of human experience, this was not their original intention. They created a search engine, and then they realized that **in the "exhaust" of the search engine, there was an enormous amount of surplus data.**

Then as the dot-com bubble burst they were attacked by their own entrepreneurs and funders, and they needed to figure out how to continue as a business. Since Sergey Brin and Larry Page were Stanford-educated postmodernists with no sense of First Principles and First Values, Brin says something like, "I didn't want to feel like a schmuck. I didn't want my

Silicon Valley place to close." They were stuck in a success story governed by win/lose metrics.

Amit Patel was the particular person who really understood it, and he worked closely with Eric Schmidt a couple of years later. **They developed an entire model in which**—because it was an unprecedented reality, and this computation structure had never existed before—**was not governed by law.**

This is the Wild West, as they would say in America.

"No one's going to stop us because no one's thought of it. We're going to basically steal your personal experience without your permission." That's the core model of Facebook, Google, Intel, Oracle, Amazon, Microsoft, and all the rest.

In different ways, they're all doing the same thing. Their business model is surveillance capitalism.

THE SIX DECLARATIONS OF GOOGLE

Here are the declarations. They're actually kind of shocking, and I'm quoting directly:

1. "We claim human experience as raw material for the taking. On the basis of this claim, we can ignore considerations of individuals' rights, interests, awareness or comprehension."

Do you get the insanity of that? For example, **you sign a waiver whenever you get a new app. It says "agree" or "disagree," and there's this long contract that would take you two hours to read that no one ever reads, which bypasses genuine consent, in which you agree to unbelievable things**.

*What you're agreeing is to have all your
data stolen and sold to third parties, but
you don't even know what you're reading.*

The average person takes fourteen seconds, according to one study, to read those contracts, which aren't really contracts. They're "un-contracts," as Zuboff calls them. **They're violations of the notion of contract.**

So back to the declarations:

1. "We claim human experience as raw material for the taking. On the basis of this claim, we can ignore considerations of individuals' rights, interests, awareness or comprehension."
2. "On the basis of our claim, we assert the right to take an individual's experience for translation into behavioral data."

Meaning: everything you did—every hovering of a mouse, every exclamation point, every question mark—is all fed into this AI monstrosity, which then uses machine learning to translate your experience into a new shadow script.

- It's a shadow script that's only readable by the new technological priesthood.
- This new text is readable only through this machine intelligence that then conducts auctions—millions or billions per second—**selling your information in order to target you for some version of manipulation unbeknownst to you, and that violates your will.**

3. "A right to take, based on our claim of free raw material, confers the right to own the behavioral data derived from human experience."

4. "A right to take and to own confer rights to know what the data discloses."

It's beyond shocking.

- ◆ 'We have a right to take your experience."
- ◆ 'We have a right to turn it into data."
- ◆ 'We have a right to own your data."
- ◆ 'We have a right to know what the data discloses."

So the personality profile generated by machine intelligence—the engine of artificial intelligence, which you're unaware is happening, that then builds a profile to manipulate you—we own that. *We have a right to know all of this about you even though you didn't give us permission.* **Why? Just because. We're just claiming it.**

It's a completely made-up claim. And **the only way you can make up a claim like this with such vicious audacity is if you have no First Principles and you have no First Values.**

INSTEAD OF SOLVING EXISTENTIAL AND CATASTROPHIC RISK, OUR BEST MINDS ARE CAUGHT IN THE SUCCESS STORY

If there are no First Principles and First Values, then:

- ◆ There is no irreducible Unique Self.
- ◆ There is no *Homo amor.*
- ◆ There is no Love as a First Principle.
- ◆ There is no interior quality that needs to be honored and supported.

"I'm not responsible for the emergence of a Unique Self Symphony. None of that's true. None of that exists. That's just a social construction of reality after all," say Larry Page, Sergey Brin, Mark Zuckerberg, and a host of others, along with tens of thousands of the best data scientists who've been absorbed into the tech plex drain.

It's a tragedy.

We need our best minds and our best scientists to solve existential risk and catastrophic risks. We need our best interior scientists, who are articulating First Values and First Principles, working with our best exterior scientists, who can develop external solutions. Exterior and interior need to move together.

But what's happening today is that the best scientists are being absorbed into the tech plex because they're being paid enormous salaries.

Each one of these scientists and their families are caught in a rivalrous success story governed by win/lose metrics. **So we're actually draining the best minds in the world in order to develop the best way to get more and more surplus behavioral data—these are behavioral futures about you that are sold against your interest.**

All of this is happening all the time. And you think that you're being benefited with "these really sweet apps," that "Google and Facebook that are really lovely because they gave you a free email account," that "they're free," and "they give you a sense of empowerment." So basically, **the world of the web is playing to your need for empowerment** and may serve you in all sorts of ways.

It's not that Facebook doesn't do many good things or that Google doesn't do many good things—of course they do. But those good things are a mask for this deeper dystopia.

FROM HOLDABLES TO WEARABLES TO BIOMETRIC SENSORS

Imagine when we go from "holdables"—you hold your phone, you hold your computer, you're downloading data—to "wearables"—which is Bluetooth or Google Glasses and all sorts of devices and clothing being made today in what's called the Internet of Things.

*We're developing more and more
what's called the Internet of Things,
which means that all of the world
will become a virtual web.*

Why do you think there's Google Earth? Why do you think there's Google FaceTime view? **These are all taking pictures of all domains of experience and feeding it into the Google plex, the Facebook plex, the Oracle plex, the Microsoft plex monster.** That's actually what's happening.

Now imagine the third level: biometric sensors, under-the-skin sensors—we're very close to that. The reason people are going to use them is because they can predict cancer in thirty years. See, all these things have good uses. Your health can be better served by biometric sensors, which are already beginning to be used around the world, meaning *an under-the-skin chip in order to give you the best health in the world—and also for you to be part of the grid, because if you're not part of the grid you don't exist: you won't be able to get a job or get insurance.*

So by that point you've got holdables (your phone, your computer), wearables (Bluetooth, your Google Glasses) and all sorts of other structures that are going to become part of what's called the Internet of Things. It's the clothing of your life, whether it's a thermostat in your house or whether it's in your bed—smartphone, smart thermostat, smart bed.

And then come the digital assistants. **It's a move to appeal to people to empower them.** *We're going to give you what the rich people have. The rich people have digital assistants. Now you're going to have a digital assistant.*

Isn't that great? **But your digital assistant, just like your smart thermostat and smart bed, is gathering data about everything that's happening and feeding that data into the system.**

Now, maybe you say that *there's a place where you can say no and not agree to share your data.* However, if you read the contract carefully it says that if you don't agree to share the data then most of the good features that make the system run well are not guaranteed or will be disabled. There's a little blackmail in the system. People spend fourteen seconds reading the contract, and *if you read the contract and say no, what you've bought actually won't work.* Wow!

Here are the last two Google declarations.

5. "A right to take, to own, and to confer the right to decide how we use the knowledge."
6. "A right to take, to own, to know, and to decide our right to the conditions that preserve our rights to take, to own, to know, and decide."

Which means *it's our decision how to use the knowledge, and it's our right to do everything we can to fight any law or any change in the status quo that would challenge our right to own your interior experience.* Does everyone get this? **The only reason this is possible**—and this is what *The Social Dilemma* and Shoshana Zuboff's **Surveillance Capitalism** missed, though they are both great works—**is if because as a society:**

- We are without a sense of Unique Self.
- We are without a sense of the value of interiority.
- We are without a sense of the unique value of your unique interior experience.
- We are without a sense of First Values and Principles of Cosmos.

FIRST PRINCIPLES AND FIRST VALUES REFUTE SURVEILLANCE CAPITALISM

With First Principles and First Values, we know that:

1. Cosmos is Evolution.

2. Evolution is growth and transformation.

3. The purpose of my life is to go through a unique trajectory of my own unique growth and transformation.

4. I need to place my attention on my interiority in order to facilitate my own deepest growth and transformation. This is my greatest joy, allowing me to give my unique gift and live my unique life.

Those are all First Values and First Principles. They're not dogma. We've spent the last ten years at the Center for Integral Wisdom working on articulating the best vision of these First Values and First Principles, and we're going to spend the next five or six years writing them into a Great Library. It has to be as perfect as it can be. But without these First Principles and First Values, Shoshana Zuboff's rage is sputtering, which means she can't quite express it—and I'm reading her intensely, because she's necessary reading. She cites the poet W.H. Auden in order to express her rage, but that doesn't take you home. Every time she tries to express *what values they are violating*, she comes up with some general, insipid, broad sentences that fall way short of true First Principles and First Values.

She's outraged, but since she's essentially a postmodernist—at least that's how she presents publicly—**she has no way to articulate her rage.**

I don't know Tristan Harris, but he's worked with some people at the center, with one of my colleagues. He's certainly a lovely young man, and he did a great job in *The Social Dilemma*, as did the people who worked with him. **But he has no articulate sense of the First Values and First Principles that are being violated.**

Your attention and the unique quality of your attention are part of the irreducible structure of your Unique Self.

- Your Unique Self is not your separate self. It's not a social construction of Reality, and it's not your Myers-Briggs test. Your Unique Self is an irreducibly unique quality of desire and intimacy.

Unless you validate uniqueness as a First Principle of Cosmos and validate the evolution of uniqueness as Unique Self—**without that depth of knowing there is no way you can object to the tech plex.** So that's the tragedy of Shoshana Zuboff: she falls short, she sputters. *The Social Dilemma* also sputters in the end—and that's what it was critiqued for. It's going in the right direction but is not based in First Principles and First Values. It's a big deal.

EXPOSING THE INNER STRUCTURE IN WHICH HUMAN EXPERIENCE IS BEING STOLEN

What I've tried to do is, number one, **to expose, to make clear, to make visible the inner structure in which human experience is stolen by the tech plex.** Colonized is too nice of a word. It's outright robbery, which is what a lot of colonization was, but I want to just call it robbery.

- It's an original sin.
- It's outright violation.
- It's a fundamental rape of an individual's interiority, but it's rape even without their knowledge.

And it's selling that interiority in a way that's misaligned with that person's essential interest.

Now, it's taken me the last decade to be able to articulate this clearly, and we're going to spend the next years writing about this. We're writing an entire volume on this particular dimension. **I hope for a lot of people, once you hear this, it's like, *Wow, I kind of knew that all along.*** That's the nature of a great insight. Now it's obvious. It's beautiful in that it's so obvious.

That's what we've called for the last five years: the reconstructive project.

The reconstructive project is to reconstruct First Principles and First Values that will help us understand the violation, and so we can then be activated against the violation.

ACTIVATION: THE DIRECT FIRST-PERSON EXPERIENCE OF REALITY COMING ALIVE IN ME

Here's the last point. I want to just play off the word "activated." You have to have a first-person experience of your value. You have to be activated.

One of the First Principles and First Values of Cosmos is what we want to call activation.

+ You can call it transformation.
+ In some of the mystical traditions, they called it "ascension."
+ In other traditions, they called it the "great descent."
+ But really what it means is that **you access directly an experience of Reality, and experience of Infinite Value lived as you.**

You transcend the limited identity of ego—you don't leave ego behind, you don't leave your separate self behind—**you evolve beyond exclusive identification with ego, and you come alive to your own inner nature.**

+ You watch Beethoven's *Ode to Joy* being played in a public square in Italy, and you're filled with this larger sense of yourself.
+ You do profound meditation.
+ You do ecstatic prayer.
+ You dance.
+ You do a practice of writing Outrageous Love Letters, but not as a mere writing practice—you're writing so that you actually *become* Outrageous Love.
+ You realize that you're lived as love.
+ You realize that you're lived as joy.

- You realize that Infinity manifested you—finitude—as a unique expression of Infinite Value itself.
- You realize that you're infinitely needed and infinitely desired, infinitely honored, infinitely intended by Cosmos, that you're both held by Infinity and that you participate in Infinity itself.

You must have a direct first-person experience. You can't have someone tell you that it's true unless they're telling you in a method that we call transmission. My hope is that you can hear in my voice the truth of this.

You don't have to work out the conceptual structure, just recognize, *oh, you can feel the truth of that*—that's the truth of Reality coming alive in you. It's non-conceptual.

It's the infinite value of you—not because you're a commodity and not because you're being sold to advertisers for personalized ads, or to manipulate your vote. No!

- You're irreducibly gorgeous. Your unique quality of intimacy, unique quality of presence, unique quality of joy, and unique story are celebrated and needed by all of Cosmos. And you disclose to Infinity a face of Herself. Wow!
- Your story needs to be fully lived and fully told and your gift fully given—because that's what it means to be alive in this world.

The direct experience of that is what—with total trembling humility— I'd love for you to feel in this moment.

Can you feel that? Let the ego go. Just scream *Yes. Yes!* My integrity is in that *Yes.* Our integrity lives in that *Yes,* friends. That's where our integrity lives. Wow!

We can't just paint an intellectual picture. We can't just engage in practice.

We have to be fully activated, fully alive. We have to become not *Homo sapiens*. We have to engage in the transformation, the apotheosis in which we literally participate in that Infinite Value.

In the last several years, in the last several weeks particularly, I've read maybe a thousand intense documents from different court cases, early Google documents, Facebook documents—and the intensity of this is beyond imagination.

We have to actually expose, deconstruct, obstruct, and stop this moment in history. We have to reshape it.

The argument against stopping it is that *it's inevitable*—but it's not inevitable.

It's only inevitable if there is no larger story.

It's inevitable if Sergey Brin and Mark Zuckerberg and Larry Page are driven by a success story governed by win/lose metrics. It's inevitable if the exponential profits of a very narrow sector, one percent of the population, drive reality.

But it's not inevitable in any other way.

- It's time for a revolution.
- It's time to stand.
- It's time to articulate policies and articulate a new direction.

Over the next year we're going to be thinking about what the policies should be, but one of the possibilities—and it's not yet formulated—**is for people just to get off social media en masse.** Wow! It's not yet an easy possibility. Social media has a lot of good to it. So how do we change social media? How do we change Facebook? How do we change Google?

The first activism, where it has to all begin, is in articulating First Values and First Principles, by coming together and letting go of our own egoic ambition and stepping into a Unique Self Symphony. We then become a cascading force of Spirit, of revolutionary joy, of audacity that becomes a revolution that changes the course of history.

That's what we have to do now.

We have to inhibit "inevitability" and articulate First Values and First Principles which are the basis for the great revolution.

Wow! Thank you for being with us. Yay!

Thank you, everyone.

CHAPTER SIX

FIRST PRINCIPLES BEYOND RANDOMNESS

First Principles 03 — November 1, 2020

BEYOND NATURAL LAW AND PERENNIAL PHILOSOPHY

What I want to do here first is to briefly read the unfolding credo of First Values and First Principles.

By way of introduction, the new Story is woven from First Values and First Principles.

We've talked about the distinctions:

- First Principles and First Values are not natural law.
- First Principles and First Values are not perennial philosophy.

First Principles and First Values are not drawn from nature. They're *anthro-ontologically* known; we know them from the clarified depth of our own interiors, interiors that are shared cross-culturally, across space and time. So in every generation we're able to access a dimension of First Principles and First Values.

These First Principles and First Values, mediated through a prism of cosmocentric consciousness, meaning we weave them together through the prism of all the best values that live in the world today at the leading edge of human development, **a new whole emerges greater than the sum of the parts**.

That whole is the new Story. That's what we're calling the new Story. That's what we're calling a global ethos for a global civilization.

FIRST PRINCIPLES AND FIRST VALUES

What are First Principles and First Values?

> First Principles and First Values are the inherent framework, the source code story which, iterated exponentially, drives the whole system.

What does that mean, and why does that matter?

I want to offer you a set of binary pairs that we've talked about in other contexts in some depth. We've talked about some thirty-five binary pairs. What we've said is **that these binary pairs are not contradictions. They move from contradiction to paradox and then even beyond paradox they move to what we're calling a sense of three-ness, a third. They merge to this higher union of trinity.** This trinity, this third, expresses something beyond important.

CERTAINTY AND UNCERTAINTY

For example, we're used to thinking about *I know* and *I don't know*, certainty and uncertainty, as a contradiction. There are, of course, entire schools of thought based on holding uncertainty, and entire schools of thought based on the dispelling of uncertainty and the affirmation of certainties.

There are, of course, dogmatic claims of uncertainty. Postmodernism is a dogmatic claim to uncertainty: *we don't know anything. The only thing we're sure that we know is that we don't know anything*, which of course is paradoxically quite a big claim to make. It is the performative contradiction inside the extreme forms of postmodernity.

There are also dogmatic claims to certainty. For example, reductive materialism in science is a dogmatic claim to certainty. And yet much premodern religion is also made of dogmatic claims to certainty.

You can trace the history of reality, for example, on the conflict between this apparent binary pair.

I wrote an essay a number of years ago called "Seven Stages of Certainty and Uncertainty," which you can find on our website at the Center for Integral Wisdom, a first grappling with this issue. When I was twenty-eight, I wrote two volumes in Hebrew. They're going to be published in English. One is called *Vadai* which means certainty, and the other is called *Safek*, which means uncertainty. I published them together in order to indicate that this binary split is wrong.

It's a false description of the nature of Cosmos.

Cosmos is this oscillation which creates a third between radical certainty and radical uncertainty.

Being able to hold both in a higher union is the mark of maturity.

It's the mark of intelligence.

It's also the mark of great love.

Great love is radically certain and is able to hold uncertainty.

So let's try and hold that.

QUALITIES OF THE THIRD FROM WITHIN LIGHT AND DARKNESS, MASCULINE AND FEMININE

Light and darkness are often considered to be a binary pair. In one classical text, Ecclesiastes 2:7, it says: "Greater is the light than the darkness." But in a rereading of that text from 2,500 years ago, a thirteenth-century rereading, it reads: "Greater is the light that *comes from* the darkness." All of a sudden, the binary pair is effaced and there's this new quality of light that comes from the darkness. That's the third. If you want to sum up Jung's *Red Book*, this is what he's talking about—he's reaching for this quality of the third, the light that comes from the darkness. Wow!

Masculine and feminine, the gendered binary pair. For many years we've talked about needing to move beyond masculine and feminine, about lines and circles and the ten qualities of the line and the ten qualities of the circle.

In 2015, we developed an instrument so you can check each quality of line or circle and how it lives in you and what's weak in it and what's strong in it and evaluate it and see where something in your life is not working because of a failure, a confusion in that quality of line or circle.

But then we realized that all the qualities of line and circle in one way or the other live in each of us, so each of us is a third.

We're neither line nor circle.

We were never only masculine or feminine.

We're a third.

It's a new quality that we called *unique gender*.

BINARY PAIRS AND THEIR THIRDS ARE A FIRST PRINCIPLE OF COSMOS

First Principles and First Values are the inherent framework, the source code story which, iterated exponentially, drives the whole system.

I want to go deep into this. I gave you a couple of examples of what we mean by binary pairs and the third that emerges beyond the binary pair. I hope that helps.

One of the First Values and First Principles of Cosmos is polarity; it's a fundamental principle of Cosmos.

As well, **the reality that the two reaches for the three, for the third, which is the process of evolution itself, is also a First Principle and First Value of Cosmos.** That's an example, but that's just by way of preface.

Now let's go to the heart of the matter today.

SHE COMES IN THREES: BEYOND RANDOMNESS AND CONTINGENCY

I want to introduce another binary pair, an unbelievably important one. We're about to make a huge source code breakthrough in thought together and in the universe story, in what we're calling the Intimate Universe and the Universe: a Love Story. Here we go. Let's stay close together.

In thought, there is a general split that's made between randomness and contingency. Read people like Daniel Dennett, who says something like, *Evolution is a random walk. Evolution is all about contingency, radical surprise. You have no idea what's going to happen.*

Generally, the reductionist materialists like Daniel Dennett point towards radical contingency, saying things like:

- It's all a surprise.
- There is no ultimate sense of order and pattern and design which is not a by-product of randomness.
- Reality is fundamentally contingent at its core.
- Evolution is a random walk.

That's one vision of Cosmos, but there's a second vision of Cosmos, which emphasizes *elegant order and design.* You've got what we'll call the spiritualists, the religionists who focus on the self-evident elegant order, the beauty and symmetry of Cosmos, the design which is obviously inherent in Cosmos. That group ignores or tries and explain away the contingency, the radical surprise, the apparent randomness.

So these two forces in culture are at each other's throats and have actually destroyed the contemporary universe story, leaving in its wake a superficial success story governed by win/lose metrics generating complicated systems, which is at the heart of the breakdown of Cosmos.

But **in order to displace that win/lose metrics story which is driving the pandemic and the current social disorder**—the gap between haves and have-nots, the extraction model, the exponential growth curve which is going to fall off—**you have to actually articulate a new Story**.

But you can't articulate a new Story because there's this apparent binary contradiction at the very heart of Cosmos:

- Is it all random and contingent?
- Or is it all symmetry, beauty, elegant order, and design?

But that's only an *apparent* contradiction.

She comes in threes. That's a first value of Cosmos. We move beyond the binary pair to the third.

In fact, you can access anthro-ontologically a direct first-person experience that *this split between random and contingent on the one hand and elegant order and symmetry on the other is a false split.* There's actually a third.

What's the third? **The third is the inherent *telos* of Cosmos.**

- There's an inherent direction to Cosmos, but that direction, that *telos* is not a set of rigid, predesigned plans.

As Henri Bergson said, God is much more than a planner. Evolution is much more than a planner. It's not preplanned.

- On the other hand, it's not utterly contingent. There clearly is *telos*, there's direction, and that direction yields symmetry, order, and design.

So how does it work? Here's the sentence: **Telos is the mediating principle between randomness and contingency on the one hand and elegant order and design on the other.**

What does that mean? What's does it mean, *telos*? What's the *telos* of Cosmos? The *telos* of Cosmos are the First Principles and First Values.

FIRST PRINCIPLES AND FIRST VALUES ARE THE *TELOS* OF COSMOS

First Principles and First Values are the *telos* of Cosmos.

The *telos* of Cosmos is not a preordained, predetermined old plan now being executed by a creator god who's fully external to Cosmos. No.

There's an inherent telos to Cosmos— and the incessant creativity of Cosmos follows that inherent telos.

Chaos theory and complexity theory are pointing to this. What's the point of chaos theory? The point of chaos theory is that underneath the chaos there's a higher order, there's a direction. What complexity theory is saying is that if you want to understand the virtually infinite, dazzling complexity of Cosmos, how it got here, this vast, complex hyper-object of Reality emerged through the exponential iteration of simple First Principles and First Values. That's how you generate the full complexity of Cosmos. Wow!

So the full order, design, symmetry, and complexity of Cosmos is generated by the inherent *telos* of Cosmos: the First Principles and First Values at play.

Now, this may all seem meta-theoretical and abstract, but it's unbelievably important, so I now want to make this anthro-ontologically real. I'll give you an example.

AUTHENTIC CONVERSATION HAS BOTH CONTINGENCY AND DESIGN

I call my friend every week. We've talked pretty much every week for about a decade. We never predesign our calls. We never send an agenda. We never design the calls. There's no plan that we're following. There's no particular syllabus. The calls are filled with surprise. They're filled with contingency. They move of their own accord. You might even be able to say that there's a dimension of real randomness to them. We could talk about almost anything.

And yet the calls have an incredible symmetry and design. If you looked at the transcript of any single call, without exception, it looks like it has such a fine, elegant design in how one theme leads to the next theme, to the next practice, to the next motif—that at the end of every encounter our hearts and minds are blown wide open.

So, are these ten years of conversation random and fully contingent?

Or are they designed with intentional symmetry?

The answer is it's a third. It's both and neither. It's something which is larger because **that's the nature of an authentic conversation.**

MESSIAH: CONVERSATION AT A HIGHER LEVEL OF FREEDOM, ORDER, AND CONSCIOUSNESS

In the original Hebrew, just to borrow one text, the realization of *Homo sapiens* as *Homo amor*, the realization of self-reflective mind at a higher level of freedom, order, and consciousness is called messiah or *mashiach*, which literally means conversation.

114

If you look carefully at the leading-edge sciences, my colleague Howard Bloom calls this a Conversational Cosmos. Howard and I have been talking for several weeks and tracking at every level of Cosmos, bringing together my body of heart-mind knowledge and his body of heart-mind knowledge, which are different. We're bringing them together and tracking from the first nanoseconds of the Big Bang from the perspective of interiors and exteriors the conversation of Cosmos. But the *terminus technicus*, the technical scientific term, from Howard Bloom, scientist and philosopher of science, is that *we live in a conversational Cosmos.*

WE LIVE IN A CONVERSATIONAL COSMOS WHICH HAS BOTH RANDOMNESS AND CONTINGENCY

That conversation, much like my conversation with my dear friend every week for ten years, is both fully random, spontaneous, free, contingent, and filled with surprise *and* has incredible elegant order, design, and symmetry beyond imagination. You see, the contradiction just disappeared. Why?

+ Because our conversations have *telos*. The Holy of Holies conversations have *telos*.
+ They have First Values and First Principles—ordinating, guiding values and principles.
+ They're very simple. They don't go to any detail.

We're committed to be together in Eros, in Outrageous Love.

We're committed to the full emergence of the radical Unique Self/*Homo amor* of my friend. The conversation is focused on her.

Those are First Values and First Principles—a *telos* or plotline, if you will— of Holy of Holies. They're the plotline of Reality. They're the inside of the inside.

They're not a preordained design and yet, just like simple First Principles in complexity theory and chaos theory, they generate symmetry, design, and beauty beyond imagination.

Wow! The *telos* of the conversational Cosmos resolves the binary contradiction between randomness and contingency on the one hand, and elegant order, design, and symmetry on the other. **Now we can begin to have a conversational Cosmos.**

We can begin to enact a new universe story based on, emergent from, the clustering together and generation of a new Story greater than the sum of the parts, emerging from First Values and First Principles.

I'll give you one last sentence. That description I gave of Holy of Holies: that level of conversation is available to all of us. In the image of the interior scientists, the enlightened one is the one whose ordinary conversation is a Holy of Holies conversation. It's a stunning idea. It's called in one language *sichat chulin*. **When ordinary conversation becomes a Holy of Holies conversation, that is to say spontaneous conversation is infused and guided by First Values and First Principles, then you create a different conversation.**

Notice that in the world today what we're missing is conversation. We've actually lost the ability to have a conversation. The reason we've lost the ability to have a conversation is because there's a complete breakdown of First Values and First Principles.

CHAPTER SEVEN

FIRST PRINCIPLES RESPOND TO EVOLUTIONARY NEED

First Principles 04 — November 8, 2020

OUR GLOBAL CIVILIZATION IS ON THE VERGE OF DEVOLVING TO A CHAOS POINT

We're in a moment of crisis. And crisis always takes place at a pivoting point when there's two roads that, as it were, diverge in the wood. We can either jump to a higher level of order, elegance, beauty, and freedom, or we can devolve into deeper suffering and tragedy.

Crisis has always been a feature of Reality. Reality operates at a plateau and then moves towards a crisis point. When the old systems sufficiently break down, when there's enough pain, enough suffering, the crisis explodes.

- The gorgeous news is that crisis is an evolutionary driver, that crisis is a birth, that crisis births the next level of possibility.
- Every civilization has met crisis.
- Every civilization was able to transmute certain dimensions of the crisis to get larger, to get deeper, to get more profound, to get wider, to get more loving.

But ultimately every major civilization has fallen.

It's a very big deal to understand that. There is no civilization that ultimately didn't fall.

Today, for the first time in human history, we're in a global civilization, so civilization is no longer a local one.

When we talk about civilization falling, we usually say:

- ◆ The great Mayan civilization fell.
- ◆ The Roman civilization fell.
- ◆ The Greek civilization fell.
- ◆ The great civilization of Kashmir fell.

But today our civilization is completely intermeshed, intertextured, inter-intermated, interdigitated. It's a global civilization.

The problem is we haven't solved the series of causations, the series of factors, the generator functions, that have generated the collapse. So the generator functions of the original collapses are still at play. We haven't solved them. So there's no reason to think in any rational manner that this civilization is going to go on *ad infinitum.*

In fact, we now understand that this vast, complicated system that we've enacted is reaching what they call in systems theory the "chaos point."

My dear colleague and friend, Ervin Laszlo, wrote a book called *The Chaos Point* to outline the precise contours of what that means: **our system is at a place on the verge of complete breakdown.**

In our global civilization we don't just have bows and arrows or even B-52 bombers. We have exponential technology that's available to many more non-state actors than ever, and that exponential technology creates exponential destruction powerful enough to destroy all of civilization—not just in its present form, but in its future form. It has the power to collapse civilization, to actually realize the sixth mass extinction.

It's because of those factors, because we have a global civilization that's now exponential, that we face the potential second shock of existence.

It's not just the death of the individual human being, which was the first shock of existence when death transformed from a biological fact to an existential experience. Now we have the second shock of existence, where **global civilization with exponential technology is now on the verge of devolving into a chaos point out of which it won't be able to liberate itself. We'll be the generation right before the sixth mass extinction.**

So how do we respond to that?

Of course, our nature is to look away from it:

- It's too big.
- It's too much.
- It's too overwhelming.
- We can't imagine the possibility, and so we deaden ourselves.
- We become numb to the shock, to the possibility of the shock.
- We turn away.
- We turn away from the unimaginable.

But if we turn away from the unimaginable, the unimaginable will become the Real.

So what we have to do is we have to turn towards. We have to turn towards, creatively, our crises of birth. Crisis is an evolutionary driver.

All of the energy that lived at the moment of the great Flaring Forth, the first Big Bang, lives in us. **And all the creative potential**—and all of the possibility and all of the promise and all of the potency—**all that lives in us.**

And so we can engage this reality and birth something undeniably new—something that not only avoids dystopia. No, we must actually enact utopia.

- You can't counter dystopia with patchwork solutions.
- You can't counter the energy of dystopia by trying to just hold things together.

You can only counter dystopia with utopia.

In other words, the unimaginable nature of dystopia has to be countered with the ability to access this quality of imagination that allows us to imagine utopia.

I want you to get the distinction. It's only the possibility of creating heaven on earth that will allow us to avoid hell on earth and the end of earth as we know it—the planet will remain, but it will be the end of the human story on planet earth.

- We need the energy of not just local problem-solving.
- We need the energy of creating a new level of civilization.
- We need the energy of self-reflective human triumph: birthing a new human, birthing a new humanity.

The essence of that activity is the enactment of First Principles and First Values.

In this new moment in time, we go back and comb through history and comb through our present, and we access what's underneath custom, underneath sociology, underneath all the surface structures, underneath all the local conflicts.

- The shared universal grammar of value that integrates the best information available in all of the exterior sciences, along with the best information available in all of the interior sciences, brings it together and says, *these are the First Values and First Principles of Cosmos.*

- Out of the thread of those First Values and First Principles, we enact a new Story.
- That new Story becomes the ground of a global ethos for a global civilization.

Now, that's a shocking accomplishment. That's what needs to be done. We need to establish those First Values and First Principles. And we need to respond to all the naysayers who say, "There is no value in Cosmos." We need to show why there is value in Cosmos, why there are First Values, and we need to weave from those First Values the new Story.

THE FIRST VALUE OF NEED

Let me give you an example of a First Value of Cosmos: the response to need. Need and the dignity of need is an example of a First Value and First Principle of Cosmos.

I have a close friend whose wife was having a very hard time. I'm quite close with both the husband and the wife. We study together and they're partners in this revolution. And the wife in this particular couple had a very bad day. So, you know, when I spoke to the husband, I said, "Wow, how was your day? You know, how was your day together?" And he said, "Oh, it was really, really kind. I found my kinder self because she really needed me," and it really struck me. It moved my heart. He understood that when **someone comes to you in genuine need, the response in honoring that need is itself a First Principle and First Value of Cosmos.**

- We respond to need.
- We are moved by need.
- It's need that always creates the next step.

We're always responding in our social policy, in our political policy, in our economic policies. We're always responding to needs—and **it's always genuine needs, authentic needs, that dictate the next step**. That's what we mean by *our crisis is a birth*.

121

Crisis means there's a genuine need.

Single-cellular life can't breed. There was an oxygen crisis several billion years ago. And so the inherent intelligence of evolution animated by First Principles and First Values responded—and one of those First Principles and Values is we respond to need. We respond to need by birthing a new reality, a new possibility, by bringing together separate parts to create a new whole the likes of which has never been seen.

> *New emergence, new possibility, and new value is always created in response to a need.*

Now, we should know that need appears in multiple forms. So one form of need is: *I exist and I'm missing something.*

I'm starving, so I need food.

So we create new possibilities in response to need, as we did in the 1960s when there was the sense of a population explosion that would cause worldwide famine within fifteen years. Many books were published in the late 1960s and early 1970s about the limits of growth, the population bomb, and impending global starvation.

None of it materialized. It didn't materialize because there was a real need. That need was a crisis of starvation, and **so we then innovated**—it was **creative innovation in response to that need.**

That's one form of need but there's a second form of need.

- ♦ A need for more intimacy.
- ♦ A need for more wholeness.
- ♦ A need for more uniqueness
- ♦ A need for more creativity.
- ♦ A need to love more and deeper.

So there are needs which are needs of lack—deficiency needs. **We need to respond to what we don't have, but there's also transcendence needs.**

- We need to transcend our present situation and go deeper.
- There are needs for more depth, for more creativity.
- There's an essential need for the pleasure of transformation.
- There's a need for ever deeper possibilities of human fulfilment.

That need for deeper fulfilment does not begin with human beings. **The need for ever more fulfilment, ever more creativity, ever more personhood, ever more interiority, and ever more wholeness, and ever more intimacy is inherent to Cosmos itself.**

Cosmos responds to need, and Cosmos affirms the dignity of need.

NEED AND DESIRE ARE INTIMATELY RELATED TO EACH OTHER

If you want to really understand need, you understand that need is always coupled with desire. Desire and need are actually part of one word: need-desires.

- What are my need-desires?
- What are my desire-needs?

My desire needs are not another ice cream cone. (Although if it's rocky road ice cream, that might be a fundamental, ultimate need, but other kinds of ice cream, no.)

But need is not ice cream.

It's my deepest, most profound existential, ethical, and erotic need.

My need to be in communion. That's not just a need—it's a desire. **Needs and desires are intimately related to each other.**

WHEN I PRAY, I CLARIFY MY NEEDS

I need to identify my most profound needs. And that's why I pray.

Prayer is a way of articulating to myself, and to the Cosmos that responds to need, the clarity of my needs.

When I pray, I clarify my needs. I clarify them for myself. The actual original Hebrew word for prayer is *pallal*, which is an original three letter root in Hebrew, which means *to reflect, to clarify my needs, to clarify my desire*. So this process of clarifying need and desire is part of the process of transformation: to know my true needs, to know my true great desires.

And then what I do is access what I've called my deepest desire. I've shared this with my beloved evolutionary partner, Barbara Marx Hubbard, and together we called it your deepest heart's desire. We wrote a document, which we'll be sharing with you over the course of the next few months, called the Wheel of Cocreation 2.0, which is this map of Cosmos. Barbara called the original version the Wheel of Cocreation.

At the center of what we call the Wheel of Cocreation 2.0, we reanimated the wheel with new understandings of evolution. Only three or four weeks before Barbara passed away, we did the final sketch on a napkin at a restaurant in Portland, and at the center of the wheel we placed desire.

Cosmos responds to my deepest need. Cosmos responds to my deepest heart's desire.

Deepest heart's desire and the dignity of need—those are First Values and First Principles of Cosmos.

124

EVOLUTION DESIRES, EVOLUTION YEARNS, EVOLUTION NEEDS

Evolution yearns to fulfil itself, to fulfil its own deepest need, its own deepest desire. That's the nature of evolution.

+ Evolution yearns.
+ Evolution desires.
+ Evolution desires more and more goodness.
+ Evolution desires, evolution needs, more and more truth.
+ Evolution needs more and more beauty.
+ Evolution needs more and more creativity.
+ Evolution needs more and more uniqueness.

This is structural to Cosmos.

Evolution desires. And it's only in affirming the dignity of need and the dignity of desire as First Values and First Principles of Cosmos that we can move through this eleventh hour.

I want to tell you something. The solutions that I've heard over the last twenty years to solve the second shock of existence, to address the potential sixth mass extinction—**the solutions that I've heard in the highest circles of policy and power are shocking.**

+ They're the solutions that involve *culling the herd*, meaning letting a huge part of humanity die.
+ They're solutions that essentially involve the enacting— and we've moving close to it—of a caste system where you have this very narrow elite and the rest of humanity who serves them.

We're going very close to that direction. **These are solutions which are dystopian and totalitarian in their very nature.**

We have a tech plex that pretends to serve us but has actually become a digital dictatorship, which is a huge mining operation—and **what's being**

mined is you. We are the natural resources of the great mining operation of the tech plex.

The tech plex mines us for information, which is then churned into data through machine intelligence and then used in order to manipulate human behavior both as consumers and as voters. That's the structure of reality today. That's where we're going.

There's no way to respond to that.

There's no way to dismantle it.

There's no way to change its direction—**unless you have First Values and First Principles.**

If you don't have that, you just have a rivalrous set of relationships.

One of the characteristics of reality that's brought down every civilization is rivalrous relationship; the success story governed by win/lose metrics. **It's only by creating non-rivalrous relationship at the core structure of reality that we can heal that which has brought down every civilization— and will certainly bring down our global civilization.**

- ◆ You cannot have rivalrous relationship and exponential technology at the center of human society and avoid the sixth mass extinction.
- ◆ But you can't articulate a vision of human flourishing based on non-rivalrous relationships without First Values and First Principles.

FIRST VALUE AND FIRST PRINCIPLE OF UNIQUENESS

So, for example, you need a First Value and First Principle of uniqueness.

Reality is moving towards irreducible uniqueness which expresses itself on the human level as Unique Self. And therefore the measure of a man, the measure of a woman, is not rivalrous relationship but the fulfilment of their unique gifts and the contribution of their unique possibility and potency and promise.

And we need to reward uniqueness. **We need to enact a global Unique Self Symphony which allows for the possibility, for the first time in human history, of non-rivalrous relationship.**

OUR FUTURE DEPENDS ON OUR ABILITY TO ARTICULATE A SHARED STORY WOVEN FROM FIRST VALUES AND FIRST PRINCIPLES

These are examples of First Values and First Principles. Without these, we are lost. And so we have to reiterate without making the same mistakes of the old perennial philosophy or the old attempts at natural law. **We have to articulate a genuine, shared story woven from First Values and First Principles that becomes the ground of the global ethos for a global civilization. Importantly, it's an evolving set of First Values and First Principles.**

Friends, there's nothing more exciting than that, right?

This is the da Vinci moment. This is the Renaissance moment.

We can't do it just by declaring it. We can't do it by creating a couple of human potential courses, or by making a bunch of new-age or fundamentalist declarations.

We have to pour our hearts and our energy into every field of knowledge, and we have to aggregate and integrate into larger wholes all the separate parts and tell this new Story.

Wow! That's the vision of *Homo amor*. That's the vision of *Homo sapiens* who triumphs as *Homo amor*, who realizes his or her identity as a unique expression of the LoveIntelligence and LoveBeauty of Cosmos.

First Values, First Principles.

- ◆ It's a time between worlds, a time between stories.
- ◆ We're da Vinci together.
- ◆ It's ours to do.
- ◆ The future literally—*literally*—depends on it.

I could not thank you madly enough for being here, for all of us holding hands together in the most urgent way, but also the most joyful way.

We are not by ourselves, alone. We are held in every moment.

That's another First Principle of Cosmos: the inherent personhood of Cosmos. The Cosmos which is intimate. **The Infinity of Intimacy that knows our name is a First Principle of Cosmos.** It's not made up. It's not a declaration. It's a validated principle of interior science.

Let's do this together.

Thank you.

CHAPTER EIGHT

INTEGRATING OUR UNIQUE SELF BY RESPONDING TO THE CALL OF OUR PAST, PRESENT, AND FUTURE SELVES

Episode 215 — November 22, 2020

IT'S ONLY A SMALL GROUP OF MADLY COMMITTED PEOPLE THAT CAN CHANGE THE WORLD

Welcome from around the world. It's so gorgeous to be with you, together as this band of Outrageous Lovers—not ordinary love but Outrageous Love, the love that's the heart of existence itself.

That's who we are: a band of Outrageous Lovers.

We are that community that Margaret Mead talked about when she said, *Don't be surprised... because it's only a small community of people madly committed to each other that ever changed the world.* **It's always communities operating on the edge, and with radical commitment.**

There's a fantastic book called *Culture Moves* out of Princeton that spends ten academic essays validating this, but it's something we know in our guts. Steve McIntosh sent this book to me after I talked about it once, and **it**

129

validates this basic intuition of Margaret Mead and this intuition that we share together.

We are a small group of committed people. For 215 weeks now, a couple hundred of us have come together live, which is the best way (and it's also fantastic if you can't make it live), and we've come together to evolve the source code of consciousness and culture, to be in this point, this chasm, this time between worlds, this time between stories. In this time between worlds and time between stories we understand that the moral imperative—just as it was in the Renaissance, another time between worlds and stories—is to tell a new story.

We are here to *tell a new Story that is not fanciful conjecture, but based on what we call a weaving of the First Principles and First Values of Cosmos.*

We need to identify those First Principles and First Values that live in us anthro-ontologically. Anthro: human being. Ontology: for real.

They live in us for real. *The mysteries are within us.*

Once we access them in ourselves we can actually locate the First Values and First Principles in Cosmos. Once we identify the First Values and First Principles in this post-postmodern move, in this metamodern move, in this space where we're actually able to move beyond all the deconstructions of postmodernity and modernity, we can begin the great reconstructive project where we gather these shared First Values and First Principles, we weave them together into the new Story of Value.

OUTRAGEOUS LOVE, THE MOST POWERFUL AND INTELLIGENT FORCE IN REALITY

The new Story is not fanciful, and it's not conjecture—it's the best integration of First Values and First Principles mediated through a prism of cosmocentric love—love for All-That-Is, love that is not ordinary love but Outrageous Love.

We've ontologized love. And we have only just begun.

Who remembers John Paul Henry? It's a famous scene in American literature in which John Paul Henry is in a famous battle and he says, "We have not yet begun to fight."

So we can say: **We have not yet begun to love.**

The Bastille will fall—that is to say, all the prisons and all the contractions that stand against the freedom of Outrageous Love transforming Reality as its most powerful and intelligent force. All of that has to fall, but it's going to fall only if we come together as this madly committed band of freedom fighters—we're fighting for freedom—of revolutionaries, of evolutionaries.

As Rumi says, "Don't love ordinary, love mad." So we talk to each other about loving madly.

Don't love ordinarily—love outrageously.

- It has to have the rage of the prophet, who says, "We've got to break down the walls."
- It has to have the outrage of that which is enormous and wild and daring and steps—beyond all the timid, flaccid, placid moves of the ordinary.

We have no time for that, friends. We only have time for Outrageous Love, and we're a band of Outrageous Lovers. It's not mere human sentiment but the heart of existence itself, an Outrageous Love that moves throughout all of Reality.

So that's who we are: a band of Outrageous Lovers. We come together every week. Some of what we say is in some of the books that have begun to come out in the Great Library, but much of what we do, most of what we do, is: *we're pushing the edge here together.* That's what we're going to do today. We're going to try and break open new realities. Most of what we do here,

FIRST PRINCIPLES AND FIRST VALUES

the ground of it, is in some of the Great Library books that have already come out: Barbara's *Conscious Evolution*, my books *Your Unique Self, Self, Radical Kabbalah*, and the *Tears* book. But for the most part we're actually coming together and loving each other so much that She comes alive—She meaning the heart-throb of Reality, the LoveIntelligence of Reality, the heart-math of Reality—comes alive.

We are formulating the next steps, the new source codes.

Just like exterior science has its principles, its equations like e = mc², we are formulating together the principles of a shared language, a shared interior science.

That's what we're going to be doing today.

FROM THE PERIPHERY, WE STEADILY SUFFUSE CULTURE WITH THE NEW STORY

What's our intention? Our intention is to be the band of Outrageous Lovers. We are at the edge of culture, but we're so committed to each other. As things which are generally ephemeral rise and disappear—a bunch of likes on Facebook, something goes viral and disappears—**we are steady**.

- Every week we open our hearts again.
- Every week we blow our hearts open.
- Every week we reach and we hold each other and we go deeper in and we articulate the source code.

Then we bring it all together in new pamphlets and new books and we stay, we stay, we stay, **until that edge, that periphery of culture begins to suffuse all of culture itself**. That's the only way it ever changes.

We are telling a new Story, based on First Values and First Principles as the thread that weaves the new Story, with radical commitment.

A lot of people make a lot of sacrifices to make this possible in a million ways. We're inviting everyone to join.

132

This is not ours. It's yours. There is no me and you here. *It's us. It's we.*

It's an evolutionary "we-space." It's a revolutionary "we-space." Wow!

IT'S CRAZY GOOD TO BE TOGETHER IN THIS UNIQUE MOMENT IN TIME

It's crazy good to be with you. Can we just breathe for a second? Who can feel that experience of being together? It's mad love. It's crazy good.

This week has never happened before. And it's never going to happen again.

It's just like there's a Unique Self, the irreducible quality of consciousness awake in you particularly, this new self-recognition of the Divine. When you recognize yourself, Divinity/the Infinite Field has a self-recognition. When you come to your fullest Unique Self, there's then a shocking self-recognition in the heart of Divinity itself.

Just as there's a Unique Self in person, there's a Unique Self in time, a unique moment that never was, is, or will be again.

So let's blow our hearts open. **Let's love this moment open like we've never loved a moment open before.**

How deep is your love? Are we ready to play a larger game? Are we ready to play a larger game like we've never done before in this unique moment in time, in this Unique Self Symphony, as this band of Outrageous Lovers, at this moment between dystopia and utopia when we feel evolution literally coming awake and alive in us, as us, and through us as Unique Self Symphony?

We are ready to participate in the evolution of love.

EVOLUTIONARY LOVE CODE: THE PAST, PRESENT, AND FUTURE ARE FIRST PRINCIPLES AND FIRST VALUES OF REALITY

The past, present, and future are First Principles and First Values of Reality.

The past calls us, the present calls us, and the future calls us.

We are called by our past self, by our present self, and our future self. Unique Self incorporates all three.

Each call has a shadow expression and each call has a light expression.

Homo amor responds to the call of the past, the call of the present, and the call of the future in every instant of external time. Responding to only one or two of these calls generates distortion.

Clarity and sacred power only emerge from the full response to the holy trinity of past, present, and future calls.

Clarity and sacred power only emerge from the full response to the holy trinity of past, present, and future. We want to make this clear—not just meta-theoretically as the structure of Cosmos, but in your life and in my life.

What does this mean for our lives, *the call of the past, the call of the present, and the call of the future*? And why can't we be an Outrageous Lover without responding to it? Why can't I be a revolutionary without it? Why is this wildly important to what I'm going to do today, tomorrow, and the next day, both in my most intimate personal life and in the creation of the new world—the new human and the new humanity that we need to create?

THE EVOLUTION OF HOMO AMOR

Reality manifests in the first Big Bang which expresses itself as matter. Matter is alive. Matter is not dead. Matter has its own agency—if you really understand the deep teachings at the leading edges of the new sciences today. Matter has agency. Matter is alive. **Matter is animated with interiority and it self-actualizes. Matter self-actualizes into life.**

The first Big Bang is the discretion of Infinity in a point, the singularity, which then appears as the laws of Cosmos, the configuration of intimate patterns of mathematics and physics in Cosmos.

Matter appears, has its own internal agency. It's not inert matter, it's not dead matter. It's living matter. It's a living Universe. Matter self-actualizes into life, which is the second Big Bang. Matter come alive—the hills are alive with *The Sound of Music*—matter *triumphs* into life.

Life then goes through all of its stages like matter did and then triumphs into this new configuration of intimate coherence, this intensification of intimacy, the 100 trillion neurons in your brain—about as much as the amount of stars in the sky—which becomes the self-reflective human, *Homo sapiens*, which emerged between 70,000 and 200,000 years ago.

Now we're just at the leading edge of humanity as we stand poised between dystopia and utopia—our crisis is a birth. This crisis has to birth the new human and the new humanity, the fulfillment of *Homo sapiens* as *Homo amor*.

SHADOW AND LIGHT DIMENSIONS OF PAST, PRESENT, AND FUTURE

Back to the code: "*Homo amor* responds to the call of the past, the call of the present, and the call of the future in every instant of eternal time." So within eternity, meaning the eternity that lives beneath the superficial present, there's the fullness of presence of the present, and there's all of the past, and all of the future. Responding to only one or even two of these calls, either the past or the present, generates distortion. **Clarity and sacred power only emerge from the full response to the holy trinity of past, present, and future calls.**

FIRST PRINCIPLES AND FIRST VALUES

Let's see if we can get what this means. Let's take this slow. This is wildly exciting, and it could not be more intimate and more relevant. **The notion that past, present, and future are First Principles and First Values of Cosmos—what do we mean by that?** First let's access this in ourselves.

When we're young, we have an enormous sense of the future, the present moves quickly, and there's very little past. **As we get older, into our 50s, 60s, and 70s, there seems to be so much more past. We have a harder time accessing the future. So we need to learn how to access the future when we're older.**

When we're full and alive, the present seem much more rich but also more fleeting.

Every human being lives in these three dimensions of time: past, present, and future.

Now, there are shadow and light dimensions of each. For example, when Buddhism points to the monkey mind, the chattering of the mind in the present that moves and darts from thing to thing—social media was instantiated in the human mind long before there were computers, this darting chat, this stealing of attention—that's the superficial, busy present that you want to get underneath. That's the shadow of the present.

So we need to access the full liberation of the present, the full liberation of the now—what I want to call *now*ing, the verb of *now*ing, activating the now, *accessing full liberation in the fullness of the present.*

I'm getting under the shadow of the present, the monkey mind, and I'm accessing the full power, the liberation of the now, the power of the now, the ability to be fully here in the now. To say, "Here I am." (*Hineni* in Hebrew) "Here I am to the full call of the now."

Every moment contains within it both pain and healing. The healing for the pain of that moment is only in that moment.

If I'm not in the moment—if I'm lost in future speculation, in past rumination, continually rehearsing the past or filled with anxiety about the future—**I can't find the healing and wholeness of this moment.**

I also can't find *the call of this moment.*

HEARING THE CALL OF THE PRESENT MOMENT

There's a call of the present moment. The call of the present moment is the experience of Unique Self. **Uniqueness is not a cognitive structure. Uniqueness is a faculty of the Eye of the Heart.**

I had an exchange about exactly this a decade ago with Cynthia Bourgeault, who just wrote a book called *Eye of the Heart:* uniqueness is a heart quality that allows you to access the call of the present.

That's the call of the present. We're going to talk about that much more, but I just want to get it on the table. **There's the shadow of the present. And there's the glory, the dignity, the power of the present.** It lives in you. It's a First Principle and First Value that lives in you anthro-ontologically, and it's a dimension of Cosmos.

Time is real. Now, as we're going to see, there's also a dimension that lives inside of you that can get underneath time. We'll get to that later.

Within me there's the reality of past, present, and future that live in me anthro-ontologically. It's the reality of the space-time continuum. And I've got to live in between those three. Those are First Principles and First Values of Cosmos—meaning they have value.

THE PAST AS A MODALITY OF HEALING AND EROS

Let's think about the past for a second.

There's the shadow of the past where I keep rehearsing past events. Every once in a while, I'll talk to a couple. I don't do a lot anymore; I used to do a lot more, but occasionally I'm drawn in when I feel it's really important. I have a little gift I'm so thankful for, which is the ability to do a certain kind of work with couples on their relationship. Occasionally it'll burst out in the middle of a session, and they'll start arguing about something that happened seven years ago. Really? It happens more than you would think.

How many of us are caught in rehearsing the past? We can't seem to break free from the tyranny of the past.

The only true slave driver is the belief that yesterday determines today.

That's the tyranny of the past.

But there is also enormous healing power in the past.

What is the great breakthrough of contemporary psychology?

Josef Breuer in Vienna had these "hysterical" female patients who were thought to be insane, who were thought to be broken. Others thought they were possessed. Then Breuer realizes, *no, no, no, they're traumatized*. These hysterical women are traumatized by profound traumas, often of sexual abuse, in the past.

What can you do?

> *You can go into the past and re-narrate the past. You can re-enact the past. There are different ways to do heal this.*

Breuer begins to understand—and Freud who comes after Breuer—that actually *by going in and rebalancing and reconfiguring the past we can elicit from the past enormous power, enormous gorgeousness, enormous healing.* **Psychology turns the past into a modality of profound Eros and healing. Because healing means, *to make whole.***

Remember our Eros formula. Eros equals experience of radical aliveness, which also lives in me, moving towards, desiring ever deeper contact and every greater *wholeness*. So Eros and healing are the same. **We can access from the past this incredible power of healing.**

All of us, friends, have an enormous amount of unfinished business from the past, so we've got to access the past.

We're going to talk more about the sacred call of the past and the call of the present, but for now with your permission I want to look at the third call.

THE POWER AND PITFALLS OF PSYCHOLOGICAL SCIENCE AND ENLIGHTENMENT SCIENCE

Psychological science focuses on the past. It has a potent call, which is unbelievably important for healing, but it also has a shadow. The shadow of psychology is its obsessive focus on the past. **All of psychology makes the past the ultimate cause of the present.**

Psychology was critically important in introducing the healing call of the past, but what it then did was hyper-emphasize the past in a way that ultimately became destructive. So you go to a therapist and the therapist tells you, "It was your mother. It was this pattern. It was this dynamic."

That's all true, but it's partial. Psychology got lost in the past. Psychology got dominated by this tyranny of the past.

What responds to the tyranny of the past in psychological science? What we might call "enlightenment science." What does enlightenment science say?

Enlightenment science says, "Don't look at the past. Liberation is available in the present. That's the full power of the eternal now."

The problem is: *Just as psychology bypassed the full experience of True Self—the experience of the full power of the eternal present, which is alive, a living consciousness in which I participate—so too **enlightenment science ignored psychology.***

I want to track this with you. Enlightenment science said *it's all about the present.* It thinks that *by experiencing the fullness of my True Self*—the singular that has no plural, the eternal now that lives in me, as me, and through me—*I'll have then done all my work on my past.* That's not true.

You can have a powerful experience of present moment enlightenment and also be a jerk and behave terribly—because you haven't done the work on healing the traumas of the past. **You can't bypass the past.** If you only respond to the call of the present, you bypass the call of the past, and you distort.

I know some very special people who went to their enlightenment teachers, who thought that having awakening realizations, experiences of waking up, would bypass the need to do the work of psychological maturity, to do the work on the trauma, to do the work on the negative patterns, to do the work on healing the shadow. That doesn't work. **You cannot bypass the call of the past.**

At the same time, psychology bypassed the present. Psychology said, "If you reorganize the past…" By the way, there are about ten major schools of psychology and they argue along two major lines, but you can map all schools of psychology based on *what modality you use to re-narrate the past*; pretty much all of psychology says *it's all about the past.* But that's tyrannical.

Psychology has to move beyond the personal to access the wider Field.

You've got to walk in the wide places to have a full, potent experience of the human being's true nature.

Most psychology never accesses the true nature of the human being. It operates only within the frame of the separate self. Psychology is *the past of your separate self, of your skin-encapsulated ego and its patterns*, but it never accesses *the full power, living agency, ecstatic presence of your true nature, your True Self, which is the full Being consciousness of all of Reality that lives in you in this moment.*

Both psychological science and enlightenment science are true but partial.

This is really important. This is a basic idea of psychology. Ken Wilber and I are aligned on this idea. The first person who talked about waking up and growing up was John Welwood, in *Toward a Psychology of Awakening*, but we're talking about it in a very different way. You've got to be careful not to reduce something to something you heard that was similar from someone else. We're saying something in a completely new, fresh way.

We're talking about the relationship of psychological science and enlightenment science in these two different calls—how each one is mutually reinforcing, how each one has shadow.

EVOLUTIONARY SCIENCE: CALLED TOWARDS THE FUTURE

Now we're going to introduce a third dimension. The third dimension is evolutionary science.

Evolutionary science is not about the call of the past or the present. It's about the call of the future.

This is so deep. It's so beautiful.

You can't access the fullness of who you are unless you access the call of the future.

- I don't just have a past self that needs to be reorganized and reconfigured—as important as that is.
- I don't just have a present self which I need to fully enter into in order to be liberated.

- ♦ I'm called by a future self.

I not only have to recover the memory of my past; I have to recover a memory of the future. It's only the call of the future that can lift me up. **When I'm stuck in the mud, I can't be pushed out. I have to be pulled out by the vitality of the future that inheres in the present and calls me forward.**

HEARING THE CALL OF YOUR FUTURE SELF

Close your eyes and see if you can access your future self. Your future self is literally calling you this second. Your future self inheres in the present. The only voice of the future in the present is your accessing of that future self.

There's your individuated future self and there's the future self of the entire community.

There's a covenant between generations. The covenant between generations is: **In this present moment, in the fullness of this present, we commit to access the voice of future generations, and to commit to be covenanted with them.**

There's not just a covenant between the human being and Spirit. There's a covenant between Spirit across the ages, incarnate as human beings.

We have to take responsibility for the future.

We stand before existential risk and catastrophic risk, which is the possibility that there may be no future at all. If we can't hear the future self of the community in the present, then we can't respond to the overwhelming moral imperative of this moment. That's true for our collective lives, but it's also true for our individual lives.

We can't be *Homo amor* as individuals or as a community unless we can respond to our future self.

Close your eyes for a second and feel the tug of your future self.

I want to now give you, with your permission, three images.

MARK TWAIN'S DREAM

First, I'm going to read from Mark Twain's diary. In the mid to late 1800s, Mark Twain shared pieces of his diary in *Harper's Magazine*. Jeffrey Kripal writes up this story, but there are many stories like it. Twain in *Harper's Magazine* tells this story. Listen to what happens. His brother dies and here's what happened.

He's at the port in St. Louis with his brother Henry. He writes as follows in his diary. And he refused to publish this and other events like it in his life, because he was afraid of public ridicule in the mid-nineteenth century. Here's what he writes:

> "In the morning when I awoke I had been dreaming and the dream was so vivid, so like reality that it deceived me and I thought it was real."

But of course, friends, as we'll see, it was real.

> In the dream I had seen Henry my brother as a corpse.

Meaning he had died.

> He lay in a metal burial coffin case. He was dressed in a suit of my clothing and on his chest, on his breast lay a great bouquet of flowers, mainly white roses with a red rose in the center.

So Twain gets dressed and he goes on with his day and he says to himself, he writes in his diary there's obviously nothing real about this—he spends the whole day with Henry—it was just a dream.

But sadly it wasn't just a dream.

A few weeks later Henry is badly burned in a boiler explosion and is killed by accident when a young doctor gives him an overdose of opium. Now, usually the dead are buried in a simple pine coffin.

> When I came back and entered the dead room, Henry lay in that open case and he was dressed in a suit of my clothing. He had borrowed it without my knowledge during our last trip in St. Louis. And then I recognized instantly that this was my dream of several weeks before that was being precisely reproduced. There was Henry. A woman had given us $60, so we got not a pine, a wood casket, we got a metal casket. So there's Henry in a suit of my clothes in a metal casket. There was only one detail missing. There were no flowers. As I noticed there were no flowers a woman walks in with a bouquet of white flowers with a red rose in the middle and places the flowers on my brother's chest.

This is not just "one example." This is the high strangeness of all of Reality.

What you understand from this story is that **the future is already in the present**.

Now, in the late-nineteenth century people would challenge Twain, saying that maybe he was making it up, but since the late nineteenth century when Henry Sidgwick at Cambridge and William James at Harvard started their psychical research societies, we have now documented thousands of these types of stories—in which we guard against all possibilities of fraud through very rigorous investigation.

This is absolutely empirically true. To deny this you have to be a blithering idiot—I apologize. This is what William James called "radical empiricism." This is no longer in the realm of an anecdote.

There is now hard empirical evidence gathered cross-culturally that the future speaks in the past.

That's a very important piece of radical empirical information. Twain was afraid to publish it in the nineteenth century because we didn't have radical empirical data collections, so you could have easily been—as he was—accused of forgery. Now we've corrected that in the last 125–130 years.

This is hugely important. It's a big deal.

Now, come deeper with me. I'll see if I can access this with you.

MESSAGE FROM THE MASTER OF THE GOOD NAME

I want to tell you a second story. This is a story from the mystical literature. It's a different way of accessing the future.

This is a story about a particular mystical master who lived in a town in Eastern Europe called Karlin. It's still a town in Europe. There was this great master of Karlin, and in his lineage there were particular times in which one would do particular prayers. There was a time for the morning prayer, a time for the afternoon prayer, a time for the evening prayer.

But he would always break the law and do everything at the wrong time.

One day, he gathers all of his disciples and they get into his horse-driven wagon—it's called an *agalah* in the original language—and there's usually only room for a hundred people in it, but there are at least 200 people. Some are hanging on the wagon. They drive and drive, from Karlin until they get to this hamlet of Polish peasants on the outskirts of this remote region. It's midnight. You have to finish praying the afternoon prayer before the sun sets. Everyone's sleeping. But the people start to notice, the people feel that *someone's in town*, and so they begin to awaken from their sleep.

There's just one person who comes out, a man who was so old you can't even imagine, 120 years old, 150 years old, who knows.

He says, "Welcome, welcome, welcome, what can I do for you?"

The great master, Aharon of Karlin, says, "I want to pray the afternoon prayer."

He says, "Of course, here's a building, please, in this building."

He says, "No, I'm going to pray outside."

He says, "Of course." He's given full permission to pray outside in this Polish peasant village.

Oh my God, friends, holy brothers, holy sisters, **they begin to pray like you can't even imagine.** They're burning. There's like a burning fire moving in ecstasy, alive, awake in the village.

All of the Polish peasants wake up and they feel the fire and they come out with buckets of water. They think there's a real fire, and then **they realize it's an entirely different kind of fire and they join in prayer**.

The disciples of this master from Karlin and the Polish peasants are all screaming in ecstasy and praying together and storming all the heavens and opening all the gates—like it's never been before. It's unimaginable!

Then they all bring these fruits and these wines, and after they prayed they have this great feast of incredible and unimaginable rejoicing. And then it's over.

Now, friends, open your hearts. We're going to go to the inside of the inside now, to the deepest of the deep.

As they're getting ready to leave and the peasants are hugging the mystical disciples, Aharon of Karlin looks at the old man who had greeted them and he says, "*Nu,* you have a message for me, don't you?" The old man is startled and he says, "Yes, I have a message for you. Please let me tell you. I am 107 years old. One hundred years ago, on my seventh birthday a great master called the Baal Shem Tov, the Master of the Good Name, came to town. And he came also at midnight.

"He asked to pray the afternoon prayer. There was this incredible fire, and the peasants came out and they danced and they sang and they screamed in mad delight. They prayed together and then they feasted. When it was over he said to me, "Young boy, 100 years from now, in the future, someone in my lineage who's carrying on this great work will be here. Tell him I was here before, and tell him I'm with him now."

Wow!

So **when you open up into the ecstasy of the present, the future speaks in the present,** literally. You can access in the present both the voice of the past, and the Baal Shem Tov, 100 years before, moves into the future. Aharon of Karlin in the future hears the past, he's called by the past. **The past and the future merge with each other.**

The Baal Shem Tov, the Master of the Good Name, and Aharon of Karlin are both called by the same future, by the same hope.

FEELING THE TUG OF THE FUTURE

Hope is a memory of the future. *The hope of my life, the fullness of my life is my future self calling me.* My future self calls me. **My future self breaks the boundaries between present, past, and future.**

When I step out of my narrow self, my contraction, my monkey mind, and into ecstasy, into *ecstasis*:

- I chant.
- I dance.
- I sing.
- I eye gaze.
- I step into a sacred text and let my heart be blown open.
- I enter into the fullness of the ecstasy of the embodiment of the physical body or the heart or the mind.
- It all opens up and I can feel the future calling me.
- I can feel the tug of the future.

One of the great masters, beloved of Kafka, Nachman of Breslov, says in Aramaic: when you wake up the first thing you must do is you access *zichron alma d'atid*, you access a memory of the future world.

We're called, friends, by our future selves. We can't live without that call.

147

Stay with me one last step. It's so deep.

You can't heal by reorganizing the past. It's why one of the things that we're working on as an expression, part of the new story, which is to weave these First Values and First Principles into a new Story.

The First Values and First Principles are not the new story. **They're the thread from which we weave the new story**, which becomes the ground of the global ethos for the global civilization.

So you begin to see how that's true here.

- When I realize that I've got to access the future self;
- And I realize there's the future self of the personal and of the community,
- I begin to experience the covenant between generations and the call of the future which demands the fullness of my presence.

If I can't hear the voice of the future we're not going to have a future.

---

*That's the nature of existential risk.
Existential risk demands that I step out of
the present and hear the call of the future.*

But it's just as vital, as existentially critical in our personal lives. Because I can do all the therapy in the world, going from therapist to therapist and trying every modality, but I won't actually come home.

- Yes, I need to work with the past deeply and profoundly, but it won't bring me home by itself. Psychology got obsessively lost in the past.
- But I can't just access enlightenment science (the present).

- ◆ I need to also access the future. I've got to feel the call of my Unique Self.

Unique Self is the quality of the Eye of the Heart, which prospects, which anticipates, which can hear—it's the ear, the listening heart—which can access the shudder of the future, the tremor of the future in the fullness of the now.

It's not just Unique Self—it's Evolutionary Unique Self.

Evolutionary Unique Self is the call of evolution that lives in me. Barbara and I called that together our future self. That's our future self. That's the call of the future. **It's only the call of the future that can heal you.** Unlike enlightenment science which focuses on the present, psychological science which focuses on the past, evolutionary science is the call of the future self.

When I say, "I am evolution," when *Homo amor* says, "I am evolution," it means "I'm responsive to my future self, I can feel and hear the tug of the future."

When the Baal Shem Tov dances with ecstasy in Karlin, he can feel that one hundred years from now he needs to be there to hold the hands of the successor in his lineage who's going to hold that call one hundred years into the future.

So as we create together, we have to create the ground so that we're going to be able to pass this to the next generation. To create schools of activist Outrageous Lovers who will express and share and spread these First Principles and First Values and be storytellers and to tell this great new story. We each need to be storytellers through our Unique Self.

But for now I want to just conclude with this.

Unique Self is the antennae, Unique Self is the sense organ which sensually feels into the future and can hear the call of the future. Wow!

HOMO PROSPECTUS

Here's the last thing. In 2013, four psychology researchers published a heavy, academic article in the *Journal of Psychological Sciences*, in which they accessed articles from 2007 and 2008, also from academic journals in psychology, which talked about "prospection."

What's a prospector? In Europe and America and Asia there were always prospectors prospecting for gold. They were all about *they might find gold tomorrow*. There were gold rushes all over the world. So the prospector prospects for gold.

These authors then published a book in 2015. They spent $5 million researching it, and they called it *Homo Prospectus*. They challenged psychology for the first time, claiming that psychology is lost in the past and understands the human being only as an expression of the causation of the past.

I was ecstatic when I read the book, because we had been saying this for ten years, but didn't have enough evidence in learning cognition theory—they provided the evidence. So we're actually incorporating that book, *Homo Prospectus*, into our vision of *Homo amor*.

Homo amor is part of a larger vision of First Principles and First Values which tell the new Story of Value, and we are integrating all sorts of different meta-theories into this larger revision of CosmoErotic Humanism.

We are called by the future.

CAN YOU FEEL THE TUG?

With your permission, friends, here's one last little story for you. We can feel it together. If you can, close your eyes for a second and just feel the tug of your future self.

What is your future self calling you towards?

If I can, let me just tell you this story just to open up the space. Here's the story.

It's a story that ages ago came into my consciousness, about a little boy who's just been confirmed in his local church or his synagogue or his mosque, wherever it was. He's excited and he wants to buy himself a present. He goes to his big piggy bank. He has exactly the right amount of change. He goes to the neighborhood store, takes his piggy bank and puts all the change down on the counter. He has exactly the right amount of money, the right amount of coins, and he says to the storekeeper, "I want to buy that big red kite behind you." The storekeeper says, "Do you have enough money?" "I sure do." He has exactly the right amount of money—it's a miracle—and just enough money to also buy some string.

He ties the string to the kite and he goes to this huge park in the center of Constantinople where he lives—this big, gorgeous, beautiful park, and he ties the string to the kite. It's a gusty fall day in Constantinople, and the wind lifts the kite into the sky. He lets out the string a little, then more string and a little more string and a little more string—until the kite is so far away that you can't even see it. All you see is this kid running in the park on a Sunday with string in his hand.

An old man, representing the establishment of the present and all the corruptions of the past, says to the kid, "What are you doing?" "What do you mean, what am I doing?" the young boy says, "I'm flying a kite." The old man says, "What do you mean you're flying a kite? You're running with string in your hand. I don't see any kite. No one can see a kite." He says, "No, I'm flying a kite." The old man insists and says, "How do you know there's a kite?"

The boy says, "I know there's a kite, because I can feel the tug."

That's the call of the future, my friends. That's the future self. Can you feel the tug? Can you feel the tug right now calling us? **Can you feel the tug calling us into the future?**

If I lose access to the future, I fall into depression.

That's the mistake of enlightenment science.

You cannot be only in the fullness of the present and you can't just rework the past. You have to feel the tug of the future.

It doesn't matter whether you're seventy-two, eighty-nine, or nineteen. **The future might be the next afternoon or the next five years, but you can recreate the world.** The future is calling us.

Homo amor is filled with hope, because *Homo amor* experiences evolutionary possibility; the Possibility of Possibility, which is the greatness of tomorrow, the call of the future, our future self.

That's a First Principle and First Value of Cosmos.

Notice what we've done in terms of First Principles and First Values. We've taken the First Values of past, present, and future that live anthro-ontologically inside of us, that are structures of Reality, and we've taken those threads and woven them into the new Story, which, as you can see, becomes the ground for the ethos of a global civilization.

CHAPTER NINE

EMERGENCE: CALLED BY MY FUTURE SELF

Episode 216 — November 29, 2020

EVOLUTIONARY LOVE CODE: HEARING THE CALLS OF MY PAST SELF, MY PRESENT SELF, AND MY FUTURE SELF

The past, present, and future are First Principles and First Values of Reality.

The past calls us, the present calls us, and the future calls us. We are called by our past self, by our present self and our future self.

Unique Self incorporates all three.

Each call has a shadow expression and a light expression.

Homo amor responds to the call of the past, the call of the present, and the call of the future in every instant of eternal time.

Responding to only one or only two of these calls generates distortion.

Clarity and sacred power only emerge from the full response to the holy trinity of past, present, and future calls.

In this moment we're going to breathe together, and we're going to step into this vision. Let's take this next huge step, and let's create something undeniably and unbearably gorgeous and new together right now. Let's read together, wherever you are. We're breathing together.

The past, present, and future are First Principles and First Values of Reality.

The past calls us, the present calls us, and the future calls us.

We're called by our past self, by our present self, and by our future self.

My dear friend Sally Kempton—who's with us today—told me she's doing some important work in particular dimensions of this expression, which is gorgeous and so exciting.

There are three calls. There's my past self, my present self, and my future self. Unique Self incorporates all three.

Each call has a shadow expression and a light expression.

Homo amor responds to the call of the past, the call of the present, and the call of the future in every instant of eternal time because eternal time, the now, isn't what we call the present. **Eternal time is the full presence eternity that includes all the past and all the future.**

Responding to only one or only two of the calls generates distortion.

Clarity and sacred power only emerge from the full response to the holy trinity of past, present, and future calls.

We can only be in full ethos, we can only be in full delight, we can only be in full joy, and we can only heal suffering when we're responding to past, present, and future together. Let's feel into this, and let's see if we can recapitulate a little bit because it's super important to continue from where we were and to then pick up from where we are.

MATH AND SCIENCE LIVE IN US AS WE ARE COSMIC HUMANS

Human beings think not in mathematics, although mathematics is one expression of deep human thought. Mathematics lives in us, even as we live in the Cosmos, and mathematics lives in the Cosmos.

That's really important. We talked last week about science's implicit understanding of the Intimate Universe—it's unbelievably important—which is this implicit knowing that I as a mathematician, for example, can map the whole Cosmos through the mathematics moving in my mind.

The only reason the scientist can map the whole Cosmos through, for example, mathematics is because the whole Cosmos already lives in the scientist. The scientist is already intimately participating in Cosmos, and Cosmos is already literally participating in the scientist.

One of the ways we think is in mathematics, but where does mathematics live? **Mathematics lives in us and mathematics lives in the Cosmos.**

The reason human science works is because we are cosmic.

Human science wouldn't work if we weren't cosmic humans.

One of the ways we think is in mathematics, and it's one of the ways Reality thinks and feels—Pythagoras wasn't wrong when he said music is the sound, the melody, of mathematics—so the Cosmos also thinks and feels in mathematics, and music is the melody of mathematics. That's step one.

But here's step two, and now it starts to get crazy beautiful. There's a second way, an equally important way, that we think and we feel.

WE THINK AND FEEL IN STORIES

We think and feel in stories. That's actually our default, our first way in, **our first portal to deep knowing and understanding of Reality.**

There's a narrative arc. Cosmos is not just disjointed facts or chance happenstances that seem to bunch together. Cosmos is not just a place we need to transcend to get to the world to come.

- Exterior science sees no story in Cosmos.
- Religion sees no story that's of ultimate value in Cosmos—"it's a story that you've got to move beyond to touch eternity."
- *Homo amor* transcends the best of science and the best of religion and notices, for the first time, that there is a narrative arc to Cosmos.

In the framework of CosmoErotic Humanism, we call this the Four Big Bangs:

- The first Big Bang, which is the emergence of matter;
- The second Big Bang, which is the emergence of life;
- The third Big Bang, which is the emergence of the self-reflective mind;
- And the fourth Big Bang, which is the emergence of the new human and the new humanity, the triumph of selfreflective mind, *Homo sapiens*, in *Homo amor*, in this new human and new humanity, who is Unique Self and Evolutionary Unique Self.

In the deepest understanding of *Homo amor* there is a story.

Science at its leading edge, and religion at its leading edge, is stepping out of its old positions, and we're trying to articulate from within science and within Spirit this narrative arc to Cosmos. So there's a story in Cosmos. That's really important.

Story is an unbelievably important structure, and story holds value.

STORIES HOLD FIRST VALUES AND FIRST PRINCIPLES

One of the primary ways we communicate First Values and First Principles is through stories. It's wildly exciting.

We communicate First Values and First Principles through stories. And stories hold First Values and First Principles.

The First Value and First Principle we're talking about is the past, the present, and the future. The particular First Value and First Principle we're talking about is that Reality's inherent structure has past and present and future.

PSYCHOLOGICAL SCIENCE FOCUSES ON THE PAST; IT'S IMPORTANT BUT INSUFFICIENT

Psychology focuses on the past. The glory of psychology, the gorgeousness of psychology, is that it turns the past not into an irrelevant, dead time; **it turns the past into a living time, which we can enter into and find healing and transformation**. That's psychology's great gift: we turn to the past. There are about ten different modalities of psychology, but all of them agree that *we're looking at the past.* What they disagree on is *how do you enter the past to access the past as your most powerful modality of healing and transformation?*

In the original Hebrew, the word "Hebrew" comes from the word *Ivri*, which means *avar*, "past." But the word past, as is always in the original Hebrew, compresses two distinct meanings to communicate within the structure of language itself. Wittgenstein loved Hebrew from that perspective.

Within the structure of language itself, you see the nuance and the nature of Reality.

157

Story holds First Principles and First Values and languages holds First Principles and First Values.

The word "Hebrew," *Ivri*, Abraham who's the Hebrew, also means *avar*. It's the same three letters in Hebrew. *Avar* means "past." And *avar* also means "to cross over, to traverse." When I want to cross over to the other side:

+ I want to get to the other side.
+ I want to move beyond the swamp.
+ I want to move beyond the monkey mind.
+ I want to move beyond the contractions.
+ I want to move beyond the repetitive wheel of the past in which I'm stuck like a rat in a maze. Who remembers that lyric from Simon and Garfunkel? We're like a rat in a maze in that we keep following old patterns. It's a repetitive cycle.

What takes us *avar*, to the other side, is the past.

Psychology picks up on this strand, which was latent in ancient wisdom, and says *if you enter the past, that can be the portal to the other side.* There are really important psychological systems that you can enter to do work on getting to the other side.

What's the shadow? The shadow is *I'm stuck in the past*: obsession. The shadow is *I'm like a rat in a maze*, I can't get out. *After I've worked it out with this therapist for five years and they know all my stories, I'm going to go to another therapist and tell them all the stories again, and again, and again...*

Yes, healing takes a lifetime, but there's a way in which we get narcissistically lost in the maze of the past and we're trapped. We can't find our way out. We keep repeating the same cycle again and again. It's a circle that doesn't spiral. Who's been there and done that? We all have, in one way or the other.

There's value in approaching the past, and we can't get to the other side if we bypass the past. But that's not enough on its own. It's insufficient.

UNFINISHED BUSINESS

I want to add something to this in the form of a story, with permission. It's a story about unfinished business in the past.

- You can't bypass the past, but you can't get stuck in the past.
- We need to go to the past if there's unfinished business. When there's unfinished business, **it lets us get beneath the very structures of time. We can find our way back and reconfigure the past.**

That's an enormously powerful idea. It appears in Sufism in one way and in Hebrew mysticism another way, and it appears in certain forms of mystical Christianity. It's an incredibly important idea—*teshuva,* **which literally means "to return" and the implication is to return to the past.** I come back. It's a circle.

I go back to a particular moment in time in order to relive, to reexperience that moment in time—not to get stuck, but to reconfigure it and move forward.

If I have unfinished business in the past, I can't bypass it. I have to go back and engage that business.

Now, I want to tell you this story about a master who was a teacher of my teacher's teacher. His name was the holy Seer of Lublin, and they said he could see from one end of the world to another.

A man and his partner come to the holy Seer of Lublin. The man says, "I'm here with my partner and we want to have a child," and Fegela, his partner, says, "I'm desperate. I want to have a child. It's everything."

Sometimes a child is birthing a new and gorgeous project, and sometimes it's an incarnate physical child. And there are different kinds of children in the world.

This couple comes before the Great Seer of Lublin and they say, "I want to have a child."

The Seer looks at the man and he says, "You have unfinished business."

He says it in Yiddish, he doesn't use the word unfinished business.

"I see," he says. "You were engaged once before, weren't you?" He says, "Yes."

"You broke the engagement, didn't you?" He says, "Yes."

The Hasidic master says, "Wow, you're stuck. Unless the woman with whom you broke that engagement will give you a blessing to have a child, you can't have a child. Go find her."

He says, "But master, I don't know where Sarah is. How am I going to find her?"

The master says, "Go to the town of Ludmir and bring your wares. Set up shop and find her somehow there." It makes no sense to him, but he lived not far from Ludmir when he was originally engaged to this woman. He remembers the marketplace there. He gathers up his wares. He tells his wife he's going.

He travels to Ludmir and he stays there for three months. Every day he sets up his stall and sells his wares all the time wondering, *Perhaps the next customer*. Sometimes he feels someone brush him in the marketplace and he turns round thinking, *That'll be her*, but it's not, or he sees her from behind and when she turns around it's someone else. Three months go by and he looks everywhere. He's up day and night, and finally he's completely

160

dejected. He's just so sad. Obviously, he wasn't worthy. He wasn't able to find Sarah, his betrothed with whom he broke the engagement.

One time, he's packing up at the end of the day, and it's raining. Everyone's got all their stalls packed. The rain is coming down hard, and he sees a shelter and he goes underneath. There's another person there, so he moves away not to take their space.

The voice says, "Ah, you're always moving away from me, aren't you?" It was her voice; it was Sarah's voice. He says, "Sarah, I've been looking for you," and she says, "I know. You can't find me where I am." He can barely hear her. "I've been looking for you. I'm so sorry for the hurt that I caused you—what can I do to make it up?" She says, "What can you do to make it up where I am?"

But he can barely hear her, and he says, "I desperately want to have a child. Please bless me to have a child." She says, "The only way I'll bless you to have a child is I want you to go to my brother, who was going to be your brother-in-law and is now marrying off a daughter. He has no money. You've been here for three months. It'll take you all day and all night and you'll get to that place where we once lived and knock on my brother's door and bring him all the money that you made as a dowry so his daughter can set up her marriage. With that gift, I will bless you to have a child."

He can't believe it. He gets on his horse and his wagon and he begins to travel. He travels all day and he travels all night and he arrives exhausted, splattered with mud. He recognizes the road, and he gets to the door of the person who would have been his brother-in-law, and he knocks. It's been twenty-five years.

The brother doesn't recognize him. He says, "I'm here to bring a dowry for your daughter who's getting married."

He says, "Who are you? I have no money for my daughter. Why are you mocking me, knocking at my door at 2am in the morning?" He goes to throw him out and he says, "No, no, don't you understand? Sarah sent me, your

161

sister, Sarah." He now recognizes Yankele, who would have been his brother-in-law, and says, "What do you mean Sarah sent you? Sarah's been dead for twenty-five years. She died just a few weeks after you broke her heart."

He gives him the money for the dowry for his daughter. They celebrate the wedding together, and Yankele travels home. His wife conceives and they have a child, who becomes one of the great masters of hidden wisdom.

Can we feel it together? What's this story about? The story is about unfinished business.

When we have unfinished business with the past, the past blocks our future. And we can't access the present.

Unfinished business is always unfinished business with love. If someone has unfinished business with us, we have to allow them to approach us and not become misers with our forgiveness. We have to let them approach us, and we have to give them our love. We don't judge their open heart. **If they say they have an open heart, we trust their open heart.**

- We say we're willing to resolve the past.
- We give up being right.
- We give up being trapped *like a rat in a maze* in all of our yesterdays.
- We complete that unfinished business, we heal the traumas of the past, and we step full-on, friends, into the present.

ENLIGHTENMENT SCIENCE FOCUSES ON THE FULLNESS OF THE PRESENT

The second form of science is enlightenment science. In enlightenment science we step into the fullness of the present. I want to feel with you what the fullness of the present means.

The past mean *we're working with our separate self, with our personality, and we're trying to reheal and re-narrate the story of the separate self.* **In the present, we move into True Self.**

- True Self is the singular that has no plural.
- The total number of True Selves in the world is one. We all participate in that same True Self.
- True Self is the Field of Consciousness. *I step into that field and I shut my eyes and the whole world disappears.*
- All that exists is the utter depth and delight and rapture of pure consciousness.
- I realize I don't need anything from the past, and I don't need to be filled with anxiety about what tomorrow will bring.

I can just rest in the unbearable joy of the present, the eternity that resides in the present. I engage in the act of now-ing, as a verb. I'm here right now in this second. We rest. Enlightenment says, "Rest. Take refuge in the Buddha right now. Now."

All that ever exists from the perspective of Enlightenment science is the present moment. This is absolutely true. The present moment holds the memory of the past and the present moment holds the anticipation of the future, *but all that ever exists is now.* Here we are right now.

When I step into the now, my heart expands. I have the ability to time travel back into the past, but I also have the ability to take the next step. Let's take the next step together.

When I live in the eternity of the present—and remember, eternity is not everlasting time, the present is not everlasting time—**when you enter the fullness of the present, you enter the eternity that lives *beneath* time.** I'm beneath the spacetime continuum. I'm in eternity.

Feel it right now. Just access that right now. Let's do a transmission right now.

- We're in eternity.
- We're underneath the past.
- We're underneath the present.
- We're living in eternal time in this moment.
- We drop in.

I realize:

I'm not my body. If I didn't have my body, I would still be here.

I'm not my emotions. If I didn't have my emotions, as beautiful as they are, all my energy in motion, I'd still be here.

I drop my thoughts. My thoughts are moving around, but I get underneath my thoughts, underneath my body, underneath my emotions, and I realize:

- I am.
- I am desire.
- I am consciousness.
- I am the entire field.
- I am, right now and right here, fully alive, and fully awake.
- All of eternity courses through me.

I'm not my body. I'm not my emotions. I'm not my thoughts. **I am the consciousness, the love-awareness that holds my body, holds my thoughts, holds my emotions right now in this moment.** *Right now, I am.* The full eternity that resides in this moment. Wow! That's Enlightenment science.

But then we step in, we realize wow, just like there's a shadow to the past—the obsession with the past—**the shadow of Enlightenment science is that it doesn't allow me to do the healing work in the past the way I need to, and it doesn't allow me to hear the call of the future the way I need to.**

I get so entranced in the eternal present that when I experience Enlightenment in its shadow form, the present becomes the present—which is the "power of now," the way it's often described today, in books by that name—that excludes the past and excludes the future.

Be here now comes to mean *I let go of all the past and let go of all the future.*

No. I let go of the repetitive maze of the past, I let go of the tyranny of the past, but I step into the past to heal to complete my unfinished business.

And I'm also called by the future. I'm literally called by the future. The field of science that addresses the future is called emergence science.

BEING CALLED BY THE FUTURE: EMERGENCE SCIENCE

An emergent is the experience of synergy. Emergence science says: *something new emerges, which is more than the sum total of the past.* A new whole emerges that is greater than the sum total of the parts.

The gas called hydrogen and the gas called oxygen come together. Neither is liquid at room temperature. In a unique configuration, they come together and turn into water. *Water is emergent.* Water doesn't come from the past; water is the meeting of hydrogen and oxygen in the present that generates something undeniably new.

Emergence is the call of the future. There's the One, there's the many. There's the creative advance of novelty—and novelty is emergence science— evolution calls into the future.

- I'm called to the future.
- I'm delighted by the future.
- I'm ecstatic.
- I feel the energy of the future calling me.

DEATH IS NOT THE END BECAUSE WE EXPERIENCE THE URGENT NEED FOR A FUTURE

How do you know? If you're up for it, if you're available for it, with your permission, let me give a direct transmission of a knowing of the future.

How do we know that death is not real? **We know that death is not real—in the sense that it's not the end—because we experience in us, anthro-ontologically, the urgent need for a future.**

If we lose connection to the future, we're depressed. If we sense there is no future, we collapse, we commit suicide. In Japan this month—talk about a tragedy around the world—Japan's lost significantly more people to suicide in the past month than it did to Covid.

Suicide rates are rising all over the world—there were about a million last year and rising. Depression is on the rise all over the world; it's actually the fastest growing disease in the world.

Depression comes from an inability to hear the call of the future.

I'm called by my future self. I'm literally and actually called by my future self.

I have to recover not just the memory of the past to organize my life—**I've got to recover a memory of the future. I have to be able to respond to the call of that future self.**

THE FOUR-LETTER NAME OF GOD IS THE FUTURE THAT LIVES IN THE PRESENT

I'm going to tell you, with your permission, something wildly shocking. In the language Hebrew mysticism, there's a four-letter name of the divine. That four-letter name of the divine reads, in Hebrew letters: *Yud*, like a Y; *Heh*, like an H; *Vav*, like a V; then another *Heh*. *Yud, Heh, Vav, Heh*, the four-letter name of God.

- *Heh, Vav, Heh*, the last three letters, is *hoveh*, which means present.
- *Yud*, the first letter, which is a little, small letter, is the glimmer of the future. *Yud*, the first letter, is the future.

The first letter of the name of God—which is understood in the interior sciences to be the DNA of Reality—is the future, and the next three letters, *Heh, Vav, Heh,* are the present.

The name of God is the future that lives in the present.

Isn't that shocking? Literally the name of the Divine is the future that lives in the present, the future that calls in the present. Wow!

The experience of being called by the Name, my name, which is a name of the Divine—and the name of God is the sum total of all names—**is the experience of being personally addressed by the call of the future.**

The call of the future comes from my future self, and everyone has a different and a distinct call. So that experience of the future is a First Principle of Reality.

We experience Reality through the prism of the past—that's enormously important. So how does that work from an evolutionary perspective?

- The present inheres all the laws. All the breakthroughs of the past live in the present.
- Then in the present there's a creative occasion—Alfred North Whitehead calls it an "occasion"—of the present, which has received the past, and then **the future enters into the present and calls the present into the future.**

That's the nature of Reality. DNA, for example, holds codification of the future at the level of genes. It's the call of the future at the gene level of Reality. We can literally hear the call of our future selves. Wow!

The call of the future—that makes me want to stay. That's utter joy.

If you want to understand why suicide is rampant, it's because we've lost First Values and First Principles. There's no sense that *my future is intrinsically meaningful. I've already done it all. I just keep repeating the same pattern of utter futility again and again and again.*

The etiology of depression is futility,
and the etiology of suicide is depression.

It's the call of the future that makes me want to stay.

- It's not enough to go into the fullness of the present, which is Enlightenment science.
- It's not enough to be reworking the trauma of the past in a psychological sense.
- We need to step into *Homo amor* science—emergence science, evolutionary science—and hear the call of the future

PRACTICE ONE: ACCESSING THE FEELING OF CONNECTION TO THE CALL

If I lose connection to the call of my future self, I get lost in blackness and heaviness, in depression, in sadness.

Can you find that in yourself, that heaviness, that uncomfortable sense of malaise that we're not allowed to share with anyone because we're not supposed to have it anymore? But it's just always still there if we don't feel the call of the future.

- The future needs something from me.
- There's a memory of my future.
- There's a gift that I have to give.

The way I hear the call of the future
is through my Unique Self and my
Evolutionary Unique Self.

Unique Self and Evolutionary Unique Self hears the call of the future. Unique Self is a sensory organ that allows me to hear the call of the future.

In the future, I hear:

- the need of Reality for my unique being
- the need of Reality for my unique gift
- the need of Reality for my unique presence
- the need of Reality for my unique contribution

I've got to be able to discern what that is. And by the way, there's a narcissistic, separate-self expression of this: *What's my creative expression?* It's not that.

PRACTICE TWO: IDENTIFYING MY UNIQUE CALL

I want to just give you a formula, which may help you to feel into your unique gift and your unique call that comes from the future. First you have to identify:

1. *What are you really good at?* Whatever it is. Everyone's got something they're good at.
2. *What do you love doing?*
3. *What's most needed?*

In different generations there are different impetus to those three.

- Sometimes what you love most is most important.
- Other times, what you're best at is most important.
- In this generation, the third is most important: what's most deeply needed?

This is not an ordinary generation. Often, I speak to people sometimes even in our close community who talk about Unique Self, but really you can hear in the resonance **they're talking more about a separate-self ego-fulfilment of creative expression**—which is beautiful; creative expression is gorgeous—**but that's not what Unique Self is.**

169

THE UNIQUE SELF EXPRESSION OF INDIVIDUALS IN THE NASCENT STATE OF ISRAEL

I want to just give you a really great example.

When Israel was founded as a state in 1948 after the Holocaust, you had doctors and lawyers and literary writers and philosophers, and what they all did is they started farms, and drained the swamp, and created crops, and built the first factories and structures of industry—because *that was the only way that this nascent state of Holocaust survivors could actually survive.*

It was an incredibly poignant moment.

The Unique Self-expression for a writer was to be a farmer. That's why Israel was able to emerge, because everyone was responding to the call of the future in that moment.

At this moment in time, when we're poised between utopia and dystopia, what's the most effective altruism we can do? **The most effective altruism we can do is to articulate First Values and First Principles**, to participate in that process in a pivotal and key role—if we can do it, if we can take a seat at the table, if we can join the revolution in some way, and contribute something, it doesn't matter how.

- It can be through funding.
- It could be through taking on a particular project and donating time and energy—but not because it's my particular creative expression, although it will be that as well, but *because it's so desperately needed now.*

I'll just tell you a little secret. This is a dark Gafni secret: I hate writing. I don't like to write. I prefer oral teaching. If it were up to me, I would only do oral teaching, I would never write a thing. But for a series of reasons, the need of this time means I have to force myself to write.

I barely wrote anything in my twenties and barely wrote anything in my thirties and I realized *I must write because it's what we need today.* I get up every morning and I write. I don't love writing at all, but that's what's needed now.

My intuitive nature and the core of my gifts are not in writing. I want to be with gorgeous groups of people talking, hugging, laughing, singing, teaching, fully engaged all day, and instead I get up and I sit and I write. Wow!

Because there's three things: there's what you're good at, there's what you love, and there's what's needed.

If you want to do an exercise where you are right now, you can make three columns. In one column put things that you love, second column, things that you're good at, and in the third column put what's most needed. List five for each. Then circle one in each of the columns and then you'll get a sense of the call of the future.

That's one way to do it.

1. One column is what you're great at, whatever it is. It can be something very simple.
2. What you love doing means you'd do it if you weren't paid to do it. I'd do it if I wasn't paid to do it, and I if I am paid to do it, I do it a thousand times more than I'm actually paid for it; that's what I love.
3. Three is what's totally, absolutely needed at this moment between utopia and dystopia, and how I can take my seat at the table.

That's one practice and everyone can do that individually.

PRACTICE THREE: LOVE LETTER TO AND FROM YOUR FUTURE SELF

I want to end with this last practice I want to invite us to do together. We have a practice we call writing Outrageous Love Letters. It's a practice of accessing Outrageous Love in the Cosmos, feeling not the ordinary love, but the quality of Outrageous Love, or what C.S. Peirce called—and we called about a decade ago—Evolutionary Love:: the love that powers evolution moving through you. So you write not as your small, separate self but as a unique expression of the entire Field, what we call Unique Self.

And then *exaggerate wildly until you're accurate.*

We've made ourselves so small. I think of that movie, *The Shrinking Man.* We're the shrinking man and woman. We've shrunk our identities.

Remember what we said earlier? **The reason human science works is because we're cosmic humans.** So we can access not only the mathematical whole of the Cosmos. Through the interior sciences:

- We can access Value.
- We can access Divinity.
- We can access the call of our future self.

Take a few minutes now to write an Outrageous Love Letter to your future self, and then ask your future self to speak to you. Just say, "Oh my God, I need to hear you. I need to hear your voice. I want to talk to you."

Write an Outrageous Love Letter from yourself to your future self. Ask your future self to speak to you and write freely for two or three minutes— just write. Don't stop writing. Just start writing and just keep writing. Ask your future self to speak to you.

In the second step, *write an Outrageous Love Letter from your future self to you.*

1. Step one is write an Outrageous Love Letter from yourself to your future self saying, "Talk to me. Find me. I need you. I want to speak to you," and you can just write the same word time and again, "I want you. I need you. I want to speak to you. Talk to me." Just sixty, ninety seconds, but *you're really calling to your future self.*

2. Then when you finish, write an Outrageous Love Letter from your future self to you.

Part of my Evolutionary Unique Self, part of my *Homo amor*, is always my Future Self.

CHAPTER TEN

BEING PERSONALLY CALLED

First Principles 07 — December 6, 2020

INTERIOR AND EXTERIOR SCIENTISTS ACCESS
THEIR CLARIFIED INTERIORS FOR GNOSIS

Welcome. We're doing another short dive into First Values and First Principles.

First Values and First Principles are an expression of the Intimate Universe. **The fact that we can know value is because we always participate in value.**

---

*Value is a structure of Cosmos.
We know value because we're
part of that structure.*

It's in us and we're in it, and that's what we mean when we say, "I live in an Intimate Universe and the Intimate Universe lives in me."

- **Human science works because we are cosmic humans**.

Mathematics lives in the scientist and mathematics lives in Cosmos.

Professor Collingwood, a friend of Professor Harding, said about Ramanujan—the Indian prodigy who was, in the early twentieth century, at Cambridge University: "He was intimate with every integer in the universe." We're intimate with mathematics. **Mathematics lives in us and lives in Cosmos when the inner subjectivity**—the interior, infinite subjectivity of the scientist—**meets the infinite subjectivity of Cosmos in that kiss, in that mutual participatory act.**

- In the same way interior sciences are born. The interior scientist accesses value that lives *within my clarified interiors.*

And I access my clarified interiors always in three ways, through Anthro-Ontology—"anthro," the human being, "ontology," the realness of Cosmos:

1. One way is common sense. I stop, I get out of my texts, I get out of all the things that steal my attention, I go inside, and I find what I know innately: common sense. We call these Common Sense Sacred Axioms.
2. Two: contemplation. I contemplate. I gather facts from science, anthropology, sacred texts. I think, I meditate, something of that nature. It's the next level of depth.
3. The third form of anthro-ontological knowing is a deep transfigurative process such as a retreat or a journey, I can know through my own humanity that the mysteries are within us, the depth, interiority, of the realness of Cosmos. I know realness. I can disclose Reality—the facts of Cosmos—through my interior. The exterior scientist does it, and the interior scientist does it. And the interior science does it through three methods. They're actually all anthro-ontological methods: Common Sense Sacred Axioms, contemplation, and transfiguration.

Transfiguration means I go through an intense furnace of clarification.

- It might be a two-week meditation retreat.
- It might be the intensity of ecstasy.
- It might be lovemaking, which is transformative.
- It might be immersing myself in nature for three days without a watch so that I'm transfigured.

These are experiences of transfiguration.

All three of these experiences—common sense, contemplation, and transfiguration—are Anthro-ontological methods which the interior scientists and the interior scientists the world over deploy to disclose First Principles and First Values of Cosmos.

FIRST VALUE AND FIRST PRINCIPLE OF UNIQUENESS

Now I want to look at two First Values and First Principles and apply them in a particular way. The first is uniqueness and the second is personhood.

Uniqueness exists from the first nanoseconds of the Big Bang. One of the trajectories, one of the plotlines, of Reality is the evolution of uniqueness.

When a person realizes what we call your "Unique Self," which is the unique expression of the entire field lived as you, Reality having a "you" experience—not your separate self, not your talent—you've awakened to your identity as a unique emergence of the entire field, that's Unique Self.

> *The notion of Unique Self is the First Principle and First Value of uniqueness becoming alive in you at the level of self-reflective unique human mind.*

But uniqueness begins in the first nanoseconds of the Big Bang with the first elements, with the first particles, with the first subatomic particles, with the first atoms.

- Atoms have a unique atomic structure.
- Atoms discern and choose and "call out to," as it were, other atoms.

That quality of uniqueness evolves—that is, the trajectory, the plotline, the *telos* of Cosmos evolves—from matter to life to mind.

177

I find uniqueness in my own interior. I experience my own uniqueness anthro-ontologically, and then I go and locate that uniqueness in the broader cosmic context. It's not like natural law. It's not naturalistic fallacy, where I'm deriving something from nature and saying it's objective.

No, I derive it from my own clarified interiors, and then I locate it in the larger cosmic natural context.

FIRST VALUE AND FIRST PRINCIPLE OF PERSONHOOD

The second First Principle and First Value is personhood, the quality of the personal that exists all the way up and all the way down.

- Whitehead talks about the unique allurement, the proto-desire to touch and to feel uniquely, which lives even between subatomic particles.
- All the way up the evolutionary chain we have the evolution of personhood until we get to self-reflective human mind.
- Then we have the evolution of personhood through all the structure-stages of human evolutionary development.

The clarification of personhood happens between us and ourselves, and between us and others.

So personhood's a quality of Cosmos.

THE EXPERIENCE OF BEING PERSONALLY ADDRESSED BY REALITY

Emergent from the First Values and First Principles of personhood and uniqueness is what we're going to call **the experience of being called**. Reality is actually calling to me. I am personally addressed. I'm personally known.

178

Expressed in an Evolutionary Love code, we might say the human being is the messenger of God. But remember, the god you don't believe in doesn't exist. This is not the caricatured god. This is god which is the face of Spirit, the face of Eros, the face of Infinity in first, second, and third persons.

- Third person, one expression of God is all the third-person qualities of Eros: electromagnetism, the four fundamental forces, all animated by Eros that move through Cosmos.
- First person is the Force that lives in me. It's one of the things that Star Wars tried to get across, that great franchise. The Force is both third person but also it lives individually in me.
- Second person is the personhood of the Force itself, if you will, the personhood of Cosmos, which lives everywhere, which knows my name and calls me forth, and which needs me.

That's the experience of the call. The human being is the messenger of God, God meaning Cosmos, meaning the Infinite Personhood of Cosmos, calls me and says, "I need you to bring a message for me."

When we say, "I am evolution," we're not just making a secular statement, a reductionist, materialist statement. We're saying:

- The personal quality of the evolutionary impulse lives in me.
- I am the personal face of the evolutionary impulse.
- There's a message I have that no one else but me has.

That's what we mean when we say, "I am evolution." I'm called by the *LoveIntelligence* of the Cosmos to be the messenger of God. And there's nothing more tragic than to be a messenger that forgot her message.

> *The deepest knowing is that my Unique Self, my soul's code, my body's knowing, is the message.*

- ◆ I am the message.
- ◆ The message is encrypted in my body, heart, and mind.
- ◆ My very being is the message.
- ◆ The message and the messenger are one.

And learning to discern that language of the call is the first step of awakening to Homo amor. One of the qualities of Homo amor is Homo amor experiences being called. And the second step is answering the call. To be called is to be personally addressed and needed by All That Is.

It's the source of all joy, Eros, and integrity.

HEARING THE CALL TO OUR NATURAL HUMAN GRANDEUR

Psychology denies human grandeur. Psychology confuses human grandeur with grandiosity.

> *Grandiosity is contrived—it's the ego's inflation—but grandeur is in fact our true nature.*

When we deny our grandeur, when we forget to confess our greatness, we're in denial of our true nature. When we deny our true nature, we suffer, we're traumatized, we're alienated, and we collapse.

The Eros of our true nature, the full aliveness of our True Self, is the experience of the unique call that addresses us in every moment. **The call, the experience of being called**—the place where *my deep gladness meets* *the world's deep hunger,* as it was once expressed—**that experience is the truest index of my real situation.**

To not experience myself as being called is to therefore fall into depression, to be devastated, to be barely able to get out of bed, to not feel the aliveness of Eros that moves through Cosmos. Just imagine for a second, friends, that the Prime Minister or President of your country called you and said, "I'm madly in love with you," because when someone's madly in love with us, we feel personally addressed.

We have to liberate love from ordinary love to Outrageous Love.

Outrageous Love is the quality of Eros that moves through Cosmos itself that addresses us personally.

Personhood is real. It calls our name and It needs us. What She says when She calls is: "I need you. I need your voice in the melody of Reality. Without your voice, the melody of Reality is off tune. I need your instrument in the Unique Self Symphony. Without your instrument, uniquely, gorgeously played by your unique trembling, by your unique quivering, Reality is discordant at its very core."

It's not quite that there's chaos or order; it's rather than reality is *chordic*. It's a chordic reality. All these dissonant, apparently disparate voices are actually allured to each other and playing together. Without the experience of being called, I cannot be psychologically whole. I can't avoid depression because the etiology of depression is futility, and futility means *it doesn't matter, that my life doesn't really matter ultimately, that I'm just marking time in a tale told by an idiot full of sounds and fury signifying nothing.*

And that false experience of reality, that illusion, is shattered when I hear the call to greatness.

CHAPTER ELEVEN

LANGUAGE AS A PORTAL TO FIRST PRINCIPLES

First Principles 08 — December 13, 2020

HUMAN VALUE WORKS BECAUSE WE'RE COSMIC HUMANS

We're talking about First Principles and First Values of Cosmos. **At this moment of existential and catastrophic risk**—first catastrophic, then tilting into existential risk, meaning a risk to our very existence—**we need to create a shared story**.

We need a shared story woven from First Principles and First Values of Cosmos that live inside of us.

We locate them first in our own interiors. We call that the anthro-ontological method, from Anthro: human being, and ontological: for real. We don't get lost in the fallacy of natural law, which was to say *we're going to locate these principles and values in nature and then apply them to us*—that doesn't work.

The only place you can accurately locate First Principles and Values is in yourself—**n**ot in your surface self but in your clarified self. That is the deepest understanding of all the most subtle and speculative minds who engage the interior sciences as the interior physics of Cosmos.

We go inside, inside we access our clarified interior.

In our clarified interior there is value.

- ◆ We said earlier that human science works because the human being is a cosmic human.
- ◆ We then add: human value works because the human being is a cosmic human.

Just like the values in a mathematical equation are, as Einstein pointed out, as it were the great mystery of Cosmos, they're accurate because we participate in Cosmos. In the same sense, **Cosmos articulates and yields value**—Cosmos creates value: goodness, truth, beauty, uniqueness, these are values—**and we can access those values.**

Human value works because we're cosmic humans.

That's critical.

- ◆ Those values are real.
- ◆ They live in us.
- ◆ We access them anthro-ontologically.
- ◆ We clarify our interiors.

There are different ways in which we clarify our interiors, which we've talked about in the past. But **we clarify our interiors, we access the value, we then trace those values as they evolve through history, and we locate those values in nature that we originally found in ourselves.**

We don't start with nature.

We first locate those values in ourselves.

Let's say I locate uniqueness in myself as a value, and then I go back to the world of matter and I realize that at some early proto-dimension and expression of uniqueness lives in the atomic structure.

- Of course, it appears in the atomic structure differently than it appears in its awakened form at the edge of human evolution—and what we're calling the Unique Self.
- But there's a direct line from the uniqueness of the subatomic world to the uniqueness of the fully awakened human Unique Self.

That's where we are. This is First Values and First Principles.

1. First Values and First Principles are anthro-ontological: we locate them in ourselves, we clarify our interiors, we locate the value, we check that it's a universal value, we then locate it in nature and matter.

2. We then locate it in the world of life, the biosphere, we then in the human world. We can trace its evolution from the very beginning of matter through life through all the stages of humanity until we get to its fullest expression in our bodies and hearts and minds in this moment right now.

3. **Those First Values and First Principles are universal.** We articulate them, we identify them, and they become the ground of the new Story which creates the new configuration of intimacy: a shared human story where we realize *that which unites us is so much greater than that which divides us.*

4. That shared human intimacy heals the global intimacy disorder and allows us to create global coherence.

That's the First Values conversation.

For example, a subatomic particle has some dimension of choice, a proto-dimension of choice, but the subatomic particle is not having an existential crisis. They're not weighing options in that sense. It's more primal and proto-instinctual, but there is an interior experience of choosing, of reaching towards.

And that experience of choice develops.

What happens is as we move from matter which triumphs as life which then triumphs in the self-reflective mind—the first Big Bang, the birth of matter, the second Big Bang when matter triumphs as life, the third Big Bang when the biosphere of life triumphs as self-reflective human mind—as we move forward, the experience of choosing how to respond to reality becomes more and more awake, alive, and conscious.

THE EXPERIENCE OF BEING PERSONALLY ADDRESSED BY REALITY

To choose how to respond to Reality is not something that we make up.

It's not like we could do anything and so we just make up what to do—*we have 50,000 options and let's just arbitrarily choose one.* It doesn't work that way.

It's much closer to the experience of being called. There's the fact of the call that we've talked about in earlier conversations about First Principles and First Values.

One of the structures of Reality is intimacy,
and part of intimacy is being called.

Intimacy begins at the subatomic level, as separate parts come together to create a larger whole that has a shared identity. Two subatomic particles come together, they create an atom, they feel each other, they recognize each other, and they have a shared purpose. In some sense, we might say accurately that the subatomic particles are calling to each other. **Intimacy means we call to each other**.

But as that experience of intimacy awakens, the nature of the call changes.

We call each other's name. When I hear my name being called, I feel personally addressed. And that experience of the call we've now exiled to romantic love, to ordinary love. But actually, the experience of the call is the experience of Cosmos itself, the personal face of the Evolutionary Impulse, the intelligent Cosmos that decided when I should be born, where I should live, what circumstance I should be born into, and what capacities I should have. None of that was me. That was all the intention of Cosmos.

I have this experience that I was intended by Cosmos.

Once I have this experience of being intended, I get underneath that insidious sense of being accidental, which is inaccurate. After contemplation and self-reflection, I get to the accurate sense of being intended by Cosmos, I then can become available to hear the call.

It's a unique call.

And we respond to that call. Answering the call is one of the essential experiences of life. But the experience of the call is one of the qualities of the Universe.

- The First Principle is the principle of uniqueness: I'm unique, so I'm called uniquely.
- Second is the quality of intimacy: the sense of I'm felt by, I'm recognized by. That's the particular quality of personhood that lives in Cosmos.

You begin to see that you've got a bunch of First Principles:

1. Uniqueness
2. The structure of intimacy [mutuality of pathos, mutuality of recognition, mutuality of purpose]
3. Personhood

Those are three First Principles. **All three come together to birth at the human level this experience of being called.**

So, the experience of being called is rooted in evolutionary First Values and First Principles.

Do we become a First Value? No, we don't. **We're unique expressions of an entire constellation of First Values.** We have infinite value, we have irreducible value. A First Value and a First Principle is a principle and value that's universal in Cosmos that is the operating system of Cosmos itself. **It's the foundational operating system that lives in us.** We're not First Values.

First values live in us. They constitute us,
and we operate based on them.

EROS IS A META-FIRST PRINCIPLE AND FIRST VALUE OF COSMOS

Very particular words and stories are different ways of accessing First Principles.

In First Principles and First Values, you have first a meta-First Value and First Principle—which is Eros.

Reality is Eros. Eros is the intrinsic creativity of Cosmos—always creating newness.

- Eros is the intrinsic creativity of Cosmos always generating newness, always generating emergence.
- The interior of Eros is the experience of radical aliveness seeking, desiring, moving towards ever deeper contact and ever greater wholeness.

Those are two huge sentences. Those two sentences constitute the Eros formula in First Principles and First Values.

There is a set of other First Principles and First Values that cluster around Eros. For example:

- **Intimacy**, which equals shared identity in the context of otherness, plus mutuality of recognition, mutuality of pathos, and mutuality of purpose.

- **Desire** is a First Principle of Cosmos because Cosmos desires the future and Cosmos desires its needs—desire implies need. So, desire and need are First Principles of Cosmos.

- **Relationship** is a First Principle of Cosmos. Reality is evolution, reality is relationship, reality is the evolution of relationship. So, relationship is a First Principle of Cosmos.

THESE PRINCIPLES ARE FUNDAMENTAL AND NOT ISOMORPHIC

You might notice that Eros, intimacy, desire, and relationship—which we express as First Principles and First Values in a couple of formal equations and sentences—**those four seem very close to each other but they're not the same all.** This by itself is a huge understanding—they're not the same. They're not isomorphic.

Notice that there's nothing underneath these four words.

Take the word gravity: what's underneath gravity? We might talk about it from a scientific perspective, what's underneath gravity? From a scientific perspective, nothing. In other words, it's fundamental. What's underneath gravity is nothing. That's what it is. It's just fundamental. **Gravity is a fundamental quality.**

But gravity is a word that science uses to describe allurement, this quality that we've talked about so many times, this quality of allurement/attraction.

But just as gravity itself is fundamental, that same sense of allurement is fundamental.

- Allurement itself is fundamental.

189

- Desire is fundamental.
- Intimacy is fundamental.
- Eros is fundamental.
- Relationship is fundamental.

That's now five words. Eros, intimacy, relationship, desire, allurement.

I've spent a decade working on these five words and bringing them together. Each one has its own formula in these First Principles and First Values.

Each one of these words is inter-included with the other words, but they're not isomorphic; they're not the same, and they're not quite synonyms.

How do you know? It's not just from their definitions.

Their definitions are different but somewhat overlapping. I'm not going to go through all the definitions again.

So how do you know? **Just speak the word.** This is really beautiful: just speak the word.

Intimacy evokes something in me. It evokes something—and there's nothing underneath intimacy. In other words, you can't reduce intimacy. You can give other synonyms for it.

But intimacy itself evokes at a particular First Value of Cosmos.

- Desire evokes another First Value and First Principle of Cosmos.
- Allurement evokes another First Value and First Principle of Cosmos.

Are desire and allurement the same? Yes and no.

When you define desire and allurement, they're actually quite close but they evoke something different.

EACH FUNDAMENTAL WORD EVOKES A DIFFERENT QUALITY

As Foucault understood, and Derrida even more sharply, and as Wittgenstein understood—the language mystics understood it most profoundly—language is an anthro-ontological principle.

There's something fundamental in language. There are core words that are fundamental words, and they're fundamental because they evoke First Principles. Intimacy evokes one thing, desire evokes something else, and allurement evokes something else. **We've articulated overlapping definitions of each one of these, but the word itself is fundamental.**

An allurement, there's a refined quality, there's a magical enchanted quality, and in allurement there's a focus on *that which is alluring me.*

Desire is more raw. There's something more fierce in desire. It's more primal than allurement. You intrinsically and naturally feel the desire that lives in you.

In the formal definition of desire and allurement, it's not so much a structurally different definition, although I delineated the words differently. It's that they evoke those two different senses. **The word itself has resonance.**

Words have resonance. They've got a wave pattern to them. They evoke something in Cosmos.

There are certain primal words, certain basic words. When I say *intimacy is a First Principle of Cosmos*, it evokes the Intimate Universe.

I had a conversation with one of my closest friends last night about the quality of intimacy. And he didn't use the word desire; he was talking about intimacy—even though in the intimacy definition, the word desire appears. Because intimacy is Reality's experience—

191

Here's the formula: intimacy equals Reality's experience of radical aliveness seeking, desiring, moving towards ever deeper contact and ever greater wholeness.

So, the word desire comes up in intimacy because they're inter-included, but **the quality of that First Value in Cosmos is evoked by the word "intimacy" in a way that's not evoked by the word "desire."** There are primal languages, so **the quality of desire lives in the word desire**.

The word desire holds that First Value and First Principle, which is why it's critical to delineate them.

What's underneath desire? Nothing. Just like there's nothing underneath the First Principle of gravity.

In other words, as with the exterior First Principle of gravity, there's a First Principle in the interior structure which is allurement.

Gravity is a scientific word for the First Principle of allurement.

- But of course, gravity is not extra; all the scientific laws of gravitational fields add an enormous amount to our depth and understanding of allurement.
- In the end, I get to allurement. And there's nothing underneath. It's primary.

It didn't need to be there but it's a choice, it's a value of an intentional Cosmos. That's really important in terms of language. Language is one way that we hold First Principles and First Values.

A second way that we hold First Principles and First Values is through story.

STORIES HOLD FIRST PRINCIPLES AND FIRST VALUES

Stories hold First Principles and First Values. One of the First Principles and First Values of reality itself is narrative or story, the notion that there's a narrative arc to Cosmos. For example, we've pointed out is this notion that there's a narrative arc to Cosmos, which is different than science or religion.

Materialist science doesn't see a narrative arc to Cosmos. Instead, it says, "the point is there is no narrative arc. It's all random, contingent, and only chance." There's no narrative arc.

Religion is not concerned with a narrative arc, either. It says, "You're in this world in order to transcend it, to move beyond the story of this world either into enlightenment or into the next world. This world is only a crucible for the next world." But the narrative arc of Cosmos itself is not important. Even your life isn't really viewed as a narrative arc, but rather as individual choices or individual tests.

But what we're saying is that a fundamental First Principle and First Value of Cosmos is story. In story, there's a narrative arc to Cosmos. **There's a reason that the human being thinks in stories.**

That's why we go to a movie. We go to a movie because it's a story. We're transfixed by the story, the story speaks to us in a particular way, whether it's around the campfire or whether it's one of the great epics of history; whether it's a contemporary movie, or a novel.

Reality speaks in stories. So it's not surprising therefore that the First Principle and First Value of story is itself a way to convey other First Values and First Principles. That's often why we use story.

We use the story because it illuminates. The word for "story" in the original Hebrew, for example, is *sapir*. *Sapir* means *illuminated light*, and it illuminates the First Principle and First Value.

STORY AND THE PRINCIPLE OF CALLING

Let me give you one example, and it's an example of the principle of calling. Calling is an unfolding of the original First Principles of personhood, uniqueness, intimacy, and then we respond to the call. The call is the place where *our deep gladness and the world's deep need meet.*

Here's the story.

It's one of the most famous stories of calling in history.

In Islam it's the central story; in Christianity it's the central story; in Judaism it's the central story. **It's about a mythic figure**—and when I say mythic I don't mean less than historical, but more than historical—**named Ibrahim or Abraham who is called**.

Genesis 12:1: The Spirit speaks to Abraham and Spirit says, *Lekh-lekha*, go forth. But actually, the word *Lekh-lekha* literally means *go to yourself.* That's the call, and that's how the story is understood, this great story of the call.

But if you look at history a little more closely and you look at the narrative thread before Chapter 12, if you check the Hebrew and Aramaic sources of the tradition, it turns out that *there's a more complex thing happening.*

Abraham/Ibrahim has challenged a figure named Nimrod, who is the reigning king deity. Abraham has challenged his vision of reality, and challenged his worldview. **He's argued that reality is not just discrete localities, but that there's a universal set of principles**, a universal set of laws—which as John Adams, the second President of the United States said, was the foundation of modern science, this notion that there's universal principles.

Abraham is challenging Nimrod by saying:

1. *There are universal principles.*
2. *The primary demand of this one Spirit is ethics.*

The primary demand is not cultic ritual, and the primary demand is not ecstasy—the primary demand of this one Spirit that calls us is goodness. That's the birth of what Herman Cohen called "ethical monotheism"—the notion that the primary demand of Spirit is not wholeness.

Wholeness is beautiful, but we actually prefer goodness: the choice to be good. That's the story.

Nimrod doesn't like this, so Nimrod goes to kill Abraham. *You challenge the worldview—*you're an imaginal cell, the butterfly's not yet born—*Nimrod goes to kill the imaginal cell Abraham.*

That's the end of Chapter 11 of the Book of Genesis based on both the text and the commentary.

Abraham runs away. Where does Abraham go? He goes to Canaan.

If you check the storyline according to this reading of the story, God is not calling Abraham and telling him, "Go to Canaan." Abraham is running away from Nimrod, and he runs to Canaan.

So, what's this whole contrived story about a divine call? Where's the divine call? It's so beautiful, it's so gorgeous: *often calls are in disguise.* **You think you're running away but you're really being called.**

You see how beautiful that is? It's a First Principle: calls are in disguise.

"I just spent the last ten years of my life… I tried this and I tried that and I tried that and I tried that—and nothing worked.

All of a sudden, here I am and I landed in this particular place, in this particular context, and I was running away from so many things, and this is where I wound up running towards. **I thought I was running away. Really, I was being pulled towards.**"

Homo amor is able to discern the language of calling.

ONE OF THE PRINCIPLES OF CALLING IS THAT CALLS ARE OFTEN IN DISGUISE

Calls are often in disguise, and this rereads the whole story. Abraham realizes only in retrospect that he's being called. Here's the first practice.

The first practice always is to take a look at your life and ask, *what was I running away from?*

I thought I was running away.

- It might have been a divorce.
- It might have been a job that didn't work out.
- It might have been—God forbid—a fall of some kind.
- It might have been some other dimension of my life.

There was something in my life that I interpreted as part of the natural pattern, but in fact it was the call. **That realization**—that the call is in disguise—**is the story of Abraham**. That's one principle.

DISCERNING BETWEEN AUTHENTIC CALLS AND COUNTERFEIT CALLS

The second principle is that there are also counterfeit calls. One principle is calls are in disguise, the second principle is you have to discern between the authentic call and the counterfeit call. For example, the jihad terrorist who goes to blow up a school bus filled with children experiences themselves as being called, but it's a counterfeit call. The ability to discern between the counterfeit and the authentic is essential.

Let's not talk about the extreme of the jihad extremist, let's talk about the human being who's on the right track, but *gets caught in their own sense of calling*. This happens often in the human potential movement, in the New Age movement, and also in the classical religions.

I want to tell you a story to capture this guiding characteristic of this First Principle of calling. There was a Hasid named David of Lilov. Every year, he would go to visit his master, Israel, the Master of the Good Name. When they would come together, you can't imagine the sparks that flew, the fire in their eyes, the ecstasy as their souls merged and brought evolutionary transformation to the inter recesses of the deepest and highest places, in the lower waters and the higher waters, when David of Lilov would meet with the Baal Shem Tov. He would go to meet him once a year on a particular holy day.

One year, he was traveling towards his master for that holy day, *Yom Kippur*, the Day of Atonement. Some hundred kilometers from the Baal Shem Tov's town of Międzybóż, the axle of the wagon breaks and the wagon sinks to the mud, near a particular hamlet, a particular *shtetl*. The people who live in the town are celebrating that particular holy day. They're ecstatic, and they all gather around them.

There's only a few of them, and they say, "We need ten people according to the Great Law to form a quorum to offer the great prayers on this great day, and we have only nine. We were praying for a miracle. We were praying that somebody would join us, so we'd be able to come together and offer the special and beautiful prayers on this holy day. Please, don't fix your wagon yet—we'll fix it for you after this. We promise we'll fix it, but just please stay with us." David of Lilov says, "I would like to, but I can't because I'm going to visit my master, Israel, Master of the Good Name. When we come together, when our souls meet, bliss erupts in the highest world and transformations take place all the way up and all the way down. I would like to stay and I'd like to help you, but I can't stay. I'm so sorry."

They're devastated, "Please..." But David says, "I can't stay." Reluctantly, they fix the axle of his wagon, and he travels on and makes it before sunset to Międzybóż. He goes to greet Israel, Master of the Good Name, ecstatic that he's made it. But Israel, the Master of the Good Name turns away from him, refusing to look on his countenance and for the entire twenty-four hours of that holy day. Four days later, another festival starts which goes for eight days, the Festival of Tabernacles, and for those eight days, Israel, the Master of the Good Name would not look at his most vaunted and prized and beautiful student, David of Lilov.

David is devastated. This great meeting, this great *hieros gamos*, this great union has been ruptured. He doesn't know what he did. He did everything to get there, to make it to be there. The holy days are over, and David of Lilov desperately begs the assistant to the Baal Shem Tov to please give him five minutes to speak to his master before he has to travel home, or he'd be devastated the entire year. The master agrees—he gets only five minutes. David of Lilov comes into the inner sanctum where his master is sitting, and his master has tears streaming down his cheeks. He says, "Master, what did I do? Our great union didn't happen. Did you turn away from me? Why?" He says, "David, David, don't you understand that generation after generation your soul reincarnated so that you could finally come to that little hamlet seventy kilometers from Międzybóż that required a tenth person so they could have a quorum to offer the prayers, and you said *no* to them. **You turned away and you kept traveling to meet what you *thought* was your destiny.**"

> *We think our Unique Self, our destiny, the call, is over there. But it's not. It's in the places where we least expect.*

Sometimes it's in being the tenth person for the quorum in that little hamlet, seventy kilometers from Międzybóż.

Calls are not only disguised, we have to beware of counterfeit calls.

Often the counterfeit call is what we think is the call to great destiny. We think *the call of great destiny is the only way we're going to be fulfilled, only if we respond in that particular way.* But that's often not the true call.

198

The call may be to be that tenth person, that person in a band of Outrageous Lovers who's uniquely needed in a unique place in a unique way at a unique time, giving whatever unique gifts are needed, maybe just to show up and stand there at the time of prayer to be the tenth person and complete the missing piece.

Sometimes we look for calls in all the wrong places. Calls are available in the everyday, in the ordinary, and the non-grandiose.

Notice that both the principles we articulated were encoded in the language of story: the story of Abraham and the story of Israel, the Master of the Good Name and David of Lilov. We tell stories because they allow us to feel the depth and the quality of the First Principle and the First Value.

We all experience our call.

It's the mark of the evolutionary, that *I experience myself as being personally addressed by Reality.*

- I am the subatomic particle, I am evolution come awake to itself.
- I am the third person of the Eros of Cosmos living uniquely in me, and all the four fundamental forces of physics live in me: the strong and weak nuclear, the gravitational, and the electromagnetic.
- I am personally addressed, madly loved, desperately needed, called by Cosmos itself.

Thank you so much everyone.

CHAPTER TWELVE

DIAGNOSING THE TECH PLEX: FROM DIGITAL DICTATORSHIP TO DIGITAL INTIMACY, FROM SOCIAL SELF TO UNIQUE SELF, FROM SOCIAL HIVE TO UNIQUE SELF SYMPHONIES

First Principles 09 — January 31, 2021

EVOLUTIONARY LOVE CODE: THE UNIQUE SELF IS UNDER ATTACK BY THE TECH PLEX

The Unique Self is the inward space of uniquely lived experience in which meaning is discovered.

The Unique Self is under attack in multiple ways, including the assumption of Big Tech and Big Data that the human being is no more than a Social Self, the assumption of the spiritual traditions that the human being is either a True Self or an Obedient Self, and the shared assumption of the entire rest of the world that the human being is a separate self.

The cultivation of Unique Self consciousness is the overriding moral imperative of this moment in history.

THE ARTICULATION OF UNIQUE SELF CONSCIOUSNESS IS THE OVERRIDING MORAL IMPERATIVE OF THIS GENERATION

I want to spend a couple of minutes on Unique Self consciousness. For now, I just want to state or say it, and then widen the lens and see **the three primary ways that Unique Self is challenged**, and **why the Unique Self is the single most important idea in the world today to alleviate suffering**; to bring hearts together, to move beyond polarity, and to respond to the existential risk, which is quite literally the death of our humanity—because we actually cease to be human beings in the deeper sense of what a human being means—and the physical death of humanity itself.

SEPARATE SELF, SOCIAL SELF, TRUE SELF, AND UNIQUE SELF

What is Unique Self?

- Unique Self says that the human being is not merely a separate self. I'm not just a skin-encapsulated ego.
- I'm also not merely a Social Self. I'm not merely in a web of social relationships.
- I'm also not merely True Self: One with Consciousness beyond my personal story. My true essence is not only an impersonal participatory part of the One.

Each of those has relevance, and each of those is important.

I'm not just separate self, but there is a dimension of a human being that's separate; separation lives in the mind of God. That's my sense of being individuated. There's some truth to that, but it's partial; I'm much more than a separate self. I actually don't exist independently of the All. I'm a unique emergent of the All. I don't exist independently of everything. I am nothing without everything. I'm dependent on it all, and it all lives in me, as me, and through me.

At the same time, I'm not just a Social Self. I'm not just a node in a network that's affected by all of the prior causes. I'm more than that.

I'm also more than pure consciousness. I'm not just awareness or awareness of awareness, as the Enlightenment traditions try to tell us. Yes, I am awareness underneath my body, underneath my emotions, and underneath my thoughts. There's still an eye, and a dimension of that eye is awareness. So I'm not just my thoughts, I'm not just my emotions, and I'm not just my body. I am—that's True Self—but I'm not just that.

I'm not just a separate self, I'm not just a Social Self, and I'm not just a True Self—I'm a Unique Self.

UNIQUE SELF: I AM IRREDUCIBLY VALUABLE AS A UNIQUE EMERGENT OF THE WHOLE

Unique Self says that on the one hand, I have a dignified separate self story that's absolutely true, but that separate self story is not all I am.

I'm also one with the Field of Consciousness, but not just the Field of Consciousness. I'm one with the Field of Consciousness, Desire, Eros, and Intimacy. The Field of Consciousness is alive. It's teeming with Eros, intimacy, and desire. But I'm not just one with that Field, I'm a *unique expression* of that Field; I'm a unique emergent, unlike any other.

I'm both part of a social web, and I'm a separate node in that social web. But I'm not just separate—I'm one with the web; the entire web in some sense lives in me, and all of consciousness lives in me.

- I'm affected by the whole thing,
- I'm a unique emergence of the whole thing,
- I am irreducibly valuable as a unique emergent of the whole thing.

That's the quality of person that's Unique Self.

YOUR UNIQUE SELF IS YOUR UNIQUE RESPONSE-ABILITY TO REALITY

My uniqueness lives in an evolutionary context. **I'm a unique expression of the evolutionary impulse itself that beats in me, and my deepest heart's desire is the desire of evolution itself.**

That's Unique Self, and it's the answer to the question, *Who are you?*

I'm going to state the Unique Self formula, and with that context, we're going to dive into our topic. If you're new and you've never heard the Unique Self context, this is a very short statement of it. If you've been with us for a decade, it's getting newer and newer all the time. **It doesn't get older; it develops every single time we express it, every single time we experience the realization again.**

Unique Self is the answer to the question of *who are you?*

> *You are an irreducibly unique expression, or emergent, of the LoveIntelligence and LoveBeauty that is the initiating and animating Eros of All-That-Is; that lives in you, as you, and through you; that never was, is, or will be ever again, other than through you; and as such, you have unique capacities; and you have unique capacity to give your unique gift and live your unique story that's needed by all that is; to give your unique gift that's needed in your unique circle of intimacy and influence, to live the unique pleasures of your life;* ***and to fulfill your unique responsibility, your unique ability to respond to Reality.***

That's very deep.

Your Unique Self is not just Reality acting on you.

That's the Social Self. The Social Self says, "Reality acts entirely on you." There's a great sentence in *Walden Two*, B.F. Skinner's utopian novel about what society should be, and in many ways the basis for the worldwide web.

FROM DIGITAL DICTATORSHIP TO DIGITAL INTIMACY

We'll get to that in a couple of seconds, but I'll just give you one sentence. Frazier, the lead character in *Walden Two*, says: *You have to set up certain behavioral processes which will lead the individual to design his own good conduct. We call that sort of thing "self-control." But don't be misled, control always rests in the last analysis in the hands of society.*

Meaning: "You actually don't act upon the world. You think you do, but you don't. The world acts upon you."

Unique Self says *No!* to that.

- Unique Self says that you have a unique response-ability.
- Your Unique Self is your unique response to Reality.
- And that response is generated internally.

Because the Field of Consciousness and Desire lives uniquely in you— and therefore, you're not merely responding to the cues that you've received through various forms of nudges and social pressures—**you're actually acting on Reality from within**. The world may appear to act on you, but you actually act on the world.

Your unique response to Reality—that's your Unique Self. That has irreducibly unique value: your response to the world, your gift to the world, and your unique way of living and being.

YOUR UNIQUE SELF HAS IRREDUCIBLE VALUE AND IS YOUR CURRENCY OF CONNECTION

Even if you don't have a job in thirty years because machine intelligence has obsoleted most of the jobs:

- You have a Unique Self.

- You have a unique gift.
- You have a unique way of living, laughing, loving, and being.
- There's a poem only you can write.
- There's a song only you can sing.
- You have a unique set of insights.
- You have a unique quality of intimacy,
- You have a unique configuration of desire that's you.

That's the essence of Unique Self: irreducible value.

Through mastering the instrument of your Unique Self, you actually don't alienate yourself, because Unique Self is not separateness. You realize that **uniqueness is not the structure of alienation; uniqueness is the currency of connection.**

Uniqueness joins you with, and uniqueness makes you a part of. Your Unique Self instrument allows you to play your instrument in the Unique Self Symphony.

So now we have a narrative of intimate communion. That's our context. That's Unique Self.

B.F. SKINNER: THE HUMAN BEING IS A SOCIAL SELF

Now I want to try and go deep with you, because we have to diagnose correctly what's actually happening.

By the way, somebody mentioned Brené Brown. She is doing a decent job, and I think she's making a great contribution in terms of healing shame.

However, she stops talking about shame at a surface level of separate self. She does a good job at the psychology of separate self, but doesn't access the qualities of the True Self, Unique Self, or the evolutionary context: Evolutionary Unique Self or Unique Self Symphony. So she's doing a very good job at organizing separate self, but level one. But it's a great level and she's doing a great job at level one. So more power to you, sister!

Now what I want to try and share with you is something so dramatic, so shocking, and so disturbing. We're going to respond to it—the revolution has to respond to it.

It's a moral imperative to transform this dimension of Reality.

There was a very well-known behavioral psychologist named B.F. Skinner, who was at Harvard for several decades. Skinner talks about a set of ideas which were profoundly attacked and condemned in very fundamental ways. Chomsky wrote a very famous essay reviling Skinner. The reason is because **in the way Skinner was understanding Reality, he understood the human being as being primarily what I'm calling**—echoing Skinner—**a Social Self**. Skinner basically says the human being is only a Social Self.

He talks about this in a book called *Beyond Freedom and Dignity* and in *Walden Two*, his utopian novel published after World War II. Skinner is actually coming from a very important place; he's misread and misunderstood. **He's absolutely wrong because the human being is much more than a Social Self, but where he's coming from is very important.**

B.F. SKINNER: LET'S NULLIFY THE AUTONOMOUS MAN, THE INNER MAN

I want to read you a passage from Skinner, from *Beyond Freedom and Dignity*. Skinner says:

> We need to abolish the autonomous man—the inner man, the possessing demon, the man defended by the literatures of freedom and dignity—his abolition has long been overdue.

207

He has been constructed from our ignorance, and as our understanding increases, the very stuff of which he is composed vanishes, and it must do so to prevent the abolition of the human species. To man qua man—this autonomous man, this inner man—we say good riddance. Only by dispossessing him can we turn from the inferred to the observed, from the miraculous to the natural, from the inaccessible to the manipulable.

This is an incredible paragraph.

For example, Shoshana Zuboff, in *Surveillance Capitalism*, quotes this paragraph in horror, but her horror is both correct and incorrect. She doesn't fully understand Skinner's motivation and where he's coming from. So what does Skinner say in this paragraph?

What Skinner basically says is that we need a technology of social behavior.

But why does Skinner say it? Chomsky attacks him, and Zuboff is aghast; correctly so. Skinner is basically saying *let's nullify the autonomous man and let's nullify the inner man.*

SKINNER'S APPROACH—NULLIFYING THE AUTONOMOUS MAN—IS THE BASIS OF SOCIAL MEDIA

Now we're going to show that Skinner is the basis of social media—the basis of Facebook, the basis of Google—and that **there's a direct line between behaviorism and Skinner, and Surveillance Capitalism and the tech plex.** Once we realize that, we understand what's animating the web, and therefore understand how we have to respond: to deconstruct the web as it exists now and create an entirely new vision of what the web needs to look like.

We need to create a Facebook, but it has to be a Unique Self Facebook.

We're going to draw a direct line from Skinner to Facebook, and we're also going to take issue with the people who critique Skinner, like Shoshana Zuboff, without actually understanding his motivation. **Her failure to understand his motivation and provide an alternative enormously weakens her critique of the web** in *Surveillance Capitalism*—and makes actually ineffective in the end. Just like the important movie *The Social Dilemma, Surveillance Capitalism,* doesn't actually understand the web, or the underlying structure and motivations of the people who were trying to animate it that way. So they simply reviled and dismissed them.

Shoshana Zuboff reviled Skinner. She realizes his relationship to the worldwide web, but doesn't understand its motivation. We've got to go much deeper.

Let's go super deep. We're literally breaking new ground in culture now, and we have to madly step in. So here we go.

First, Skinner is a utopian—we've got to get that straight. He realizes that we need to recast society. Because in the 1950s, 1960s and the 1970s, and even as early as before World War II, Skinner realizes that we're facing existential risk; he is one of the first to really get existential risk. This is something that Zuboff completely misses. In the passage which I just read, what does he say? He's talking about creating a technology of behavior *in order to prevent the abolition of the human species.*

What is the abolition of human species? That's existential risk. That's what he's talking about.

In his introduction to *Walden Two*, his utopian novel, he places himself in the lineage of those who tried to offer new narratives of human identity. So he talks about Buddha, and he talks about Thoreau. In other words, **Skinner, in *Walden Two*, is trying to reformulate human identity.**

Why? Although Skinner places himself in the general lineage of new formulators of narratives of identity, he doesn't directly use Buddha's work in any direct way—but Skinner gets Buddha's critique of the separate self. **Skinner's books *Beyond Freedom and Dignity* and *Walden Two* are based on the threat of existential risk and the realization that existential risk is going to come from a separate self gone berserk.** This is exactly what the Buddha was afraid of.

Buddha says, "The thinking that I'm only a separate self is an illusion, but that illusion creates *duḥkha*, or suffering." So Skinner says, *Yes, in Buddha's time, that illusion created suffering. But in our time*—as he watches the emergence of nuclear power, as he now adds that exponential technology, which creates exponential risk—*the separate self doesn't just create duḥkha, but the separate self is going to destroy reality. Actually, together with exponential technology and nuclear power, the separate self will be the abolition of human society entirely.*

That's what Skinner is talking about.

Skinner realizes the threat of existential risk pretty much before everyone else did, and he's saying that the way to respond to existential risk is to formulate a new vision of the human being.

C.S. LEWIS VS SKINNER: THE ABOLITION OF MAN, THE ABOLITION OF HUMAN SOCIETY

There's a book from 1943 called *The Abolition of Man*, written by C.S. Lewis. He says that the abolition of man is going to come because in forty, fifty, or sixty years—he doesn't give an exact date—**there's going to be an omnicompetent state which develops irresistible scientific technologies. That omnicompetent state is going to label themselves as the "conditioners," and they're going to attempt to socially condition human beings in order to have a engineered safe society.** Then he says, that's going to cause the abolition of man.

But by the abolition of man, C.S. Lewis means not existential risk in the sense of the death of humanity—though exponential technology, nuclear proliferation, or climate change. He's talking about the existential risk which I've been referring to which is not the death of humanity, but the death of *our humanity*.

When Lewis talks about the abolition of man, he says that **that it's going to be brought about by the conditioners, those people, in his language, who have stepped out of the Tao. By stepping out of the Tao, he means they've stepped out of the experience of living within intrinsic value structures.** They've stepped into a kind of reductive scientific materialism, which says there is no intrinsic interior value in Cosmos. C.S. Lewis talks about the Tao, this intrinsic interior value, as this form of universal natural law.

He says that if we step out of the Tao, out of this natural law which binds all human beings, what's going to happen is, in a few generations, there's going to be new technologies and the conditioners are going to appear. And these conditioners are going to initially intend to do this for the good of Reality.

That's what he says on page twenty-four, paragraph five:

> They'll initially intend the good of reality, but in the end, because they've stepped out of value—they've stepped out of the Tao, because in the end they're materialists—it's going to be the power of the few over the power of the many is they become despotic, and it's going to actually destroy human beings.

People who will be controlled and conditioned will no longer be human beings as we currently experience.

Now, when C.S. Lewis talks about the abolition of man, he says, it's going to happen through the "conditioners" developing technologies of human behavior. Who's he referring to? He's referring to Skinner, but no one notices; no one even reads the book anymore. It's an unbelievably important book, written in 1943, in the middle of World War II, as we realized the emergence of human power, and **we realized we don't have a story equal to our power.**

When C.S. Lewis talks about the conditioners who are going to cause the abolition of man, he's talking about Skinner, who views the human being as being a Social Self and as being *manipulable*, which is exactly the word Skinner uses. Lewis says, *Wow, that's the most dangerous thing in the world.* Although Skinner hadn't yet published *Beyond Freedom and Dignity*—he published that book in 1971— Skinner's basic ideas of behaviorism and the conditioners were already available; they were already in the *zeitgeist*, so Lewis was already aware of them in a meta-sense.

C.S. Lewis views the danger as being the conditioners—i.e. the behaviorists—who are formed by a kind of reductive, pseudo-materialist Neo-Darwinism; a scientistic rejection of interiors; not scientific, but scientistic and dogmatic, fundamentalist rejection of interiors; a stepping out of the Tao or stepping out of value.

He says, *this is going to cause what we're calling an existential risk to our humanity*; he calls that the abolition of man, and he faults Skinner.

Thirty years later, Skinner then says to C.S. Lewis, *you got it wrong*, and he uses the words "the abolition of human society." Of course, what he's saying is that ***those people who insist on the individual, the dignity of the separate self***, which is of course the Christian tradition and the Platonic tradition, and the Greek tradition. In other words, this is the Western tradition of the dignity and freedom of the separate self, which Skinner is ascribing to C.S. Lewis, the tradition that affirms the value of the separate self human being—and ***which is going to cause the abolition of human society***.

Notice that he uses the same phrase. So there's this hidden conversation between these two great thinkers. C.S. Lewis is saying, without mentioning Skinner, "You're going to cause the abolition of man; the death of our humanity." Then, Skinner says back to C.S. Lewis, "You just don't get it, my

212

friend. We're facing existential risk to the very existence of humanity, and that existential risk comes from the separate self."

HOWEVER MISGUIDED, SKINNER IS RESPONDING TO EXISTENTIAL RISK AND CRITIQUING SEPARATE SELF AS THE SOURCE OF HUMAN DIGNITY

Now the Western idea is that human dignity and freedom is rooted in the separate self, and this is what Shoshana Zuboff gets so excited about. She says, "How could Skinner reject the dignity of the separate self? That's crazy, you can't do that." Then he embraces the Social Self, which Zuboff views as a disaster. **She's right, it is a disaster to embrace the Social Self exclusively as your model of self.** But she doesn't get what's happening.

> *Zuboff doesn't get that Skinner is responding to something important; he's responding to existential risk.*

Skinner is not a crazy man of Harvard, he has actually adopted and up-leveled Buddhist critique of the separate self. So he's saying, Buddhist critique of the separate self is real. Zuboff, who gets that Skinner is kind of an antecedent to the web, is all aghast. She's like, *how could Skinner reject the separate self?* Because **Zuboff is standing in the tradition of Western Enlightenment, which has the separate self as the source of all dignity**; this is Chapter 5 of the *Unique Self* book.

But Skinner, although he's not quoting Buddha directly, he's phenomenologically embracing that critique of the separate self. He's saying the separate self is not the source of human dignity. That's why Skinner calls his book provocatively *Beyond Freedom and Dignity*. What does he mean?

What Skinner means is we've got to move beyond the Western notion of separate self, which if you put it together with exponential technology, it's going to destroy us. Because separate self causes *duḥkha* (suffering), but separate self with exponential technology destroys everything.

That is, separate self with exponential technology is what we've called before "rivalrous conflict governed by win-lose metrics," which is the modern success story. **That false narrative is one key generator function of existential risk.** The person who gets that is not Zuboff, writing *Surveillance Capitalism*, but Skinner who she's critiquing; he totally gets that.

What Skinner says is we need a different model of self.

SKINNER DID NOT HAVE THE TOOLS TO DEVELOP TECHNOLOGIES OF HUMAN BEHAVIOR

In 1990, Skinner died frustrated because he says, *We don't have the machines and methods to generate a technology of human behavior, and so we're going to wind up with the abolition of human society*—again, playing off of and critiquing C.S. Lewis, without mentioning him by name. He's says, *Your notion of the human being as a separate self who lives within these values structures is all very nice, C.S. Lewis, but that's a pre-modern idea, and a bad idea. It's an idea that the religions have made central, but it's actually wrong; we have got to get rid of separate self.*

Skinner dies before he's able to accomplish any of this. Lamenting, he says, *I wish I had what the physicists had.* The physicists have real mathematical equations. They can manipulate objects, and they enabled all modern science. All the progress of modern science is based on mathematical measurements done by physicists. Skinner says, *Tragically, we don't yet have mathematical models that allow us to develop technologies of human behavior, which can map the human being and relationships between human beings. So, therefore, I can't get anywhere with this.*

ALEX PENTLAND, ONE OF THE ARCHITECTS OF THE WEB, IS A DIRECT CONTINUATION OF SKINNER

After Skinner died, along comes an entire new generation of data scientists. One classic representative is Alex Pentland, who wrote a book called *Social Physics*. Pentland shared this with our friend Howard Bloom, who's a senior scholar at the Think Tank and a great thinker. Pentland said, "I'm one of the major architects of the web" in a personal conversation a bunch of years ago, when Howard's book, *The Lucifer Principle*, came out. Pentland is right—he is one of the architects of the web.

In *Social Physics*, Pentland never once mentions Skinner because that's political suicide, but **what he says is a direct continuation of Skinner**. He's actually the completion of Skinner, if you will, in the following way. Pentland says, *We now do have the machines and methods to do this. We have data science, and data science is a new mathematics. With this new mathematics, we can track the human being, and the human being is not a separate self.*

That's what Pentland states in an essay he wrote, called "The Myth of Individuality."

Pentland agrees with Skinner that we need to facilitate the death of the contemporary Western notion of individuality.

He has gaggles of doctoral students who've each started their own companies, and those companies are embedded in relationships with Google, Facebook, and the entire tech plex. They're based on the notion of a Social Self, but this Social Self now can be manipulated. These are Skinner's words: "We need to move from the inaccessible to the manipulable," but not because he wants humans to be manipulated in a bad way.

Skinner is a utopian, but he's a utopian without First Values and First Principles, and that's why he's dangerous.

- Skinner is a utopian, he gets existential risk. So he's correct in saying that C.S. Lewis was too caught up in the separate self of Western society.

215

- But where C.S. Lewis was right is that he knew *we have to live within the Tao, within frameworks of value*, whereas the materialist Skinner has stepped out of frameworks of value.

He's influenced by existentialism, logical positivism, and Neo-Darwinism. He developed behaviorism, which basically considers the human being as an "It": a Social Self that you can influence through social nudges, social cues, social pressure, through a technology of human behavior that's mathematically developed through data science. Skinner's vision in *Walden Two* is of a socially engineered society, which wants not because he's a terrible guy. He's not a Stalin totalitarian, but rather a *technocratic* totalitarian, if you will. But he's not a totalitarian in the sense that he wants to rip your soul out—not at all.

Skinner is afraid of the separate self, so he wants to organize human society in a way that's safe. He understands the risks, but he's a utopian who has stepped out of the Tao.

- That's where C.S. Lewis was right in *The Abolition of Man* when he talks about the conditioners who've stepped out of the Tao. He's referring to Skinner, and he was absolutely right.
- Skinner was also right in responding to C.S. Lewis, saying, *If you just stay with the separate self, you're going to get to the abolition of human society*, playing on C.S. Lewis's phrase "the abolition of man."

PENTLAND: DATA SCIENCE IS THE NEW PHYSICS WHICH WILL ALLOW US TO ENACT A NEW VISION OF SOCIETY

We now need to go the next step. So you've got Skinner in *Beyond Freedom and Dignity*, his major book from 1971. What does he mean when he says beyond freedom and dignity? He means that *the old notions of freedom and dignity based on the separate self will bring about existential risk, the destruction and the abolition of humanity.*

Skinner says, we've got to move to a new self, the Social Self. After Skinner dies, Alex Pentland says, without naming Skinner, that we didn't have the physics to do this, but now we have social physics. He calls his book *Social Physics*, and he talks about *data science as the mathematical structure that's going to give us this new physics that's going to allow us to enact this new vision of society.*

THE FOUNDERS OF THE TECH PLEX ADOPT THE VISION OF SKINNER AND PENTLAND

Now, who are the people that Pentland and Skinner have influenced? Who has adopted their vision? The answer, **quite literally, is the founders of the tech plex**.

Let's take Mark Zuckerberg, who says, "Our goal is creating a global community." Larry Page says, "Our goal is a societal goal. Our goal is not incremental change, but revolutionary change." If you read the inner text in some of the public texts of the founders of the tech plex, they adopt Skinner and Pentland's utopianism. Pentland is directly and personally involved, through many doctoral students who have formed companies and partnerships throughout the tech plex.

SOCIAL MEDIA ARE EXPRESSIONS OF SKINNER'S WALDEN TWO

Now here's where it gets a bit creepy. But we have to get the diagnosis in order to change it. So when you look at let's say Facebook and Google's mottos, they seem very benign and lovely:

- *"We connect people everywhere."*
- *"We organize the world's information."*
- *"We bring people closer so that they can express themselves."*

What is this? These are actually expressions of Skinner's *Walden Two*, expressions of the Social Self. **Notice that the entire Tech Plex**—all of the social media platforms, Facebook, Google, the whole story—**is built around social nudges, social cues, social pressure: likes, how many views you get, sharing personal information, etc**. So what happens? Here's the mechanism: You share your data, and Google collects your data.

It doesn't ask you for it; it decided that it has a right to it. Google has six declarations.

1. We have a right to take your data without asking you or without any real informed consent on your part.
2. We have a right to feed that data into machine intelligence.
3. We're going to get out of machine intelligence a personality profile about you, about "your inner demons;" about what moves you and drives you.
4. We own that secret text about who you are.
5. We have a right to sell that text to third parties because we own it.
6. It's sold to third parties who are misaligned with your values. It's sold by automatic machine intelligence driven auctions.

Now, **what would give Google**—and Facebook and Microsoft and Samsung and Amazon, the list goes on—**the right to think that they can take your data, which is the fruit of your personal experience**? Only what C.S. Lewis described as **a stepping out of the Tao, as a stepping out of First Values and First Principles.** Because once you step out of the Tao, then you're no longer governed; you become the conditioners that C.S. Lewis describes.

C.S. Lewis described these conditioners as having this benign smiling face, who say they're doing sweet and nice things for you, and they give you all these trinkets and free apps—Gmail and WhatsApp—and they're organizing the world's information, connecting people everywhere, and "bringing the world closer together."

But what they're actually doing is fulfilling Skinner's vision of *Walden Two* and Pentland's vision of *Social Physics*, which is based on stepping out of the Tao, out of the Field of Value.

WE NEED TO REPLACE THE UNDERSTANDING OF NATURAL LAW WITH EVOLVING PERENNIALISM, AN EVOLVING SET OF FIRST VALUES AND FIRST PRINCIPLES

Now, C.S. Lewis got the Tao partially wrong. He actually identified the Tao, or value, with natural law, which is a weak idea; natural law is not sufficient. There are a lot of weaknesses in natural law—for example, it doesn't get evolution. We have to critique natural law.

We've replaced natural law with what we're calling Evolving First Values and First Principles, which is a shared narrative of human universals that are evolving. That's really important. In that sense, it's why people like Zuboff are so afraid to embrace First Values and First Principles, because they identify them with C.S. Lewis's natural law. This is where his Christianity got him in trouble; he was too influenced by Aquinas's view of natural law, which is a mistake. Natural law is not just eternal and unchanging.

In fact, **we need to replace natural law with an evolving perennialism, an evolving set of First Values and First Principles**. That's one of the core pieces of work at the Center, to understand that there's an evolving set of First Values and First Principles. That's really important.

Let's get back to our major thread. So C.S. Lewis predicts that the conditioners will step out of the Tao, that they'll step out of First Values and First Principles. So we're going to then have a set of utopian thinkers, like Skinner and Pentland, who don't have First Values and First Principles.

What's the model of utopian thinking sans First Values and First Principles? Mao, Stalin, Lenin. Communism is precisely a utopian move, which disqualifies the Universe and says, *there are no First Values and First Principles.*

THE TECH PLEX: WE ARE ORGANIZING SOCIETY AS SOCIAL SELVES

So now what do you have? You've got Zuckerberg, Page, Brin; the entire tech plex, and its view of itself is that their *organizing society*—they talk about it all the time:

- "We are the change engine of society."
- "We, at this time of a threat, are going to create global community."

It looks very sweet, but it's not sweet; it's creepy. Meaning, there's a direct line between Skinner and Pentland and data science, which says that the human being is a Social Self—therefore, to borrow Skinner's phrase, the *human being is manipulable.*

Now, that's precisely half right. The human being is a Social Self that you can manipulate through social nudges and social cues. But that's precisely only one quarter of the human being, because **a human being is not just a Social Self.**

Skinner's critique of separate self is correct, but his conclusion is wrong.

Skinner and Pentland's reductive materialist conclusion is that the human being is not a separate self at all, but a Social Self. But that ignores an enormous amount of validated conclusion and insight, both from the exterior and interior sciences. The human being is only partially a Social Self.

The human being is not only a Social Self, but is also a True Self. **The human being is also irreducibly valuable because the human being is inseparable from the entire Field of Consciousness and Desire.** Every human being participates in the one True Self, and the total number of True Selves in the world is one. Every enlightenment science and every interior science in the world has a notion, based on direct experimentation, of a deeper self than separate self and Social Self. We call that True Self.

TRUE SELF AND UNIQUE SELF ARE IGNORED BY THE TECH PLEX

True Self is ignored by Skinner, ignored by Pentland, and ignored by the tech plex. Not only is it ignored, but **the tech plex is built on attention-hijacking. When your attention is hijacked, you don't have the ability to access the inward space of meaning and practice**. There's no possibility of focusing inwardly to realize through genuine practice your true identity, which is, *I'm not merely a skin encapsulated ego, I'm not merely the illusion of separate self*. Skinner is right about that, but that doesn't mean I'm only a Social Self; I'm also True Self. I am consciousness itself.

But I'm not only True Self, I'm actually Unique Self.

Each one of us who is True Self sees through a unique set of eyes.

I have:

- A unique perspective
- A unique quality of intimacy
- A unique configuration of Eros and desire
- A unique gift to give
- A unique poem to write
- A unique song to sing

I am an irreducibly unique expression of the LoveIntelligence and LoveBeauty that is the initiating and animating Eros of All-That-Is.

So therefore, the goal is not the social hive or the superorganism of Social Selves that Pentland and Skinner talk about. The goal is not the social hive that's manipulated by social cues, or what Pentland calls *the nervous system of the planet*, which Pentland identifies with the web.

That's not what we're going for. That's not the strange attractor of society.

UNSEEN, PENTLAND AND SKINNER HAVE FORMED THE THINKING OF THE TECH PLEX, WHICH ARROGATES TO ITSELF THE RIGHT TO YOUR EXPERIENCE

Pentland and Skinner have secretly—meaning they're not actually hiding it, but they're also not openly declaring it—formed the thinking of the tech plex and of the entire enterprise of surveillance capitalism.

The tech plex arrogates to itself the right to your experience—because they've stepped out of First Values and First Principles.

That's what C.S. Lewis was referring to when he predicted it seventy years ago. He said, "The conditioners are going to step out of the Tao, and once they step out of the Tao, then they're going to become the man-molders."

He's referring to Skinner's vision.

PERSONAL DATA IS CURRENTLY BEING USED BY MACHINE INTELLIGENCE ALGORITHMS TO COMPROMISE THE TWO BASIC IDENTITIES OF DEMOCRACY: THE VOTER AND THE CONSUMER

After Skinner dies, Pentland, along with many other data scientists, develops the mathematical models, and then says, *Hey Facebook, Hey Google, let me collect everybody's data, feed it into machine intelligence, and develop personality profiles.*

Then, based on that precise information, we'll be able to directly influence the outcome of an election, for example, because we're going to know every wavering voter, and we're going to know the unique social pressure points to exert on this group of voters to make them vote in a particular way.

We're going to know exactly how to make people buy exactly what we want them to buy.

We're going to upend the two basic human identities of democracy, which are the voter and the consumer.

Democracy is going to become a sham because there's no real voting, because all of the machine intelligence is arrayed against you to manipulate your voting choice—and you don't even know it's happening.

Machine intelligence is not minor, we're talking about technology that's so sophisticated that it's completely defeated the old machine intelligence that defeated the best chess matchers in the world in the 1990s.

An exponentially more powerful machine intelligence is arrayed against you to exert a form of behavioral engineering to impact your decision-making, both as a consumer and a voter.

This is now being deployed in democracies, and it's just the beginning.

UNDER-THE-SKIN SURVEILLANCE IS THE NEXT STEP AND WILL RESULT IN DIGITAL DICTATORSHIPS

As we move from over-the-skin surveillance to under-the-skin surveillance—deploying biometric sensors, which everyone is going to need in order to join a health system, to get insurance, or to get a job—**there's going to be so much data coming in that those who own the data will essentially create digital dictatorships.**

- There might be a veneer of democracy, but democratic elections are going to become a joke.
- There might be the veneer of an economy, but your independent decisions as a consumer are going to become a joke.

The entire drama of human decision-making is going to be upended.

THE POSTMODERN DECONSTRUCTION OF VALUE TOGETHER WITH SURVEILLANCE CAPITALISM RESULTS IN THE "CONDITIONERS" PREDICTED BY C.S. LEWIS

Now here's the paradox. In Big Tech, you have this utopianism that they've adopted from Skinner and Pentland. But because the Big Tech founders are all postmodern—meaning, value has been deconstructed and there's no belief in actual value. As Yuval Harari says in several of his books, *it's all fiction and social constructions of reality; there is no genuine Unique Self, no genuine True Self, and no irreducible human value; value is a complete human fiction.*

When you marry the postmodern worldview with surveillance capitalists of the tech plex, you get the "conditioners" who've stepped out of First Values and First Principles, creating this behavioral engineering system. Predicted by C.S. Lewis, that's the scenario that we're in now.

The response to this is to develop and share a new model of self and a new Universe Story.

People like Zuboff must get it. She doesn't quite get it yet. She justly critiques Skinner but doesn't understand that he's responding to existential risk.

People like Pentland and his data scientists must get this new model of self and a new universe story as well. **The new model of self is True Self and primarily Unique Self and Evolutionary Unique Self; the move from *Homo sapiens* to *Homo amor*.** But at the core of everything is the Unique Self model.

We have to infuse the tech plex—the data algorithms of the nervous system of the planet—with Unique Self. Unique Self has to be the animating energy of the nervous system of the planet.

WE NEED TO RESPOND TO SOCIAL SELF WITH UNIQUE SELF

We need to respond to social self with Unique Self. We need to respond to reductive materialism with the Universe: A Love Story, the Amorous Cosmos. These new narratives and this evolution of the source code is essential.

That evolution of the source code needs to then infuse the source code of the data algorithms that are now hijacking authority in society today. Authority in society today is moving from governments to algorithms— but algorithms are written by human beings, and human beings are being downloaded into algorithms. **But the value that's been downloaded into algorithms is the social self, the postmodern or "social construction" values of Skinner and Pentland, all the way through the tech plex.** So when we read Google and Facebook's lovely slogans, we realize, *Oh my God, this is Skinner in disguise.*

The response is the radical downloading of Evolutionary Love, of Homo amor, of Unique Self, of the Amorous Cosmos, of the Intimate Universe, into the tech plex. This takes us from digital dictatorship to digital intimacy.

The digital world is not the enemy. The hijacking of attention for the sake of social control is the enemy.

POWER AND PROFIT, TOGETHER WITH UTOPIANISM SANS FIRST PRINCIPLES AND FIRST VALUES

Now in this last piece, let's notice one more insidious dimension of the tech plex that we can't miss: **These surveillance capitalists have married the**

direct profit and power motive. Meaning Sergey Brin, Larry Page, and the whole gang, have tens and tens of billions of dollars of individual net worth, because **they've profited from harvesting your data in violation of the First Principles and First Values of personhood**.

There's this immense greed motive, there's this immense power and profit motive, and they've married with utopianism in the tech plex—without First Values and First Principles.

Surveillance capitalism is absorbing all of your personal experience as data bits, pouring them into machine intelligence, then constructing your personal personality profile—using data science, mathematical algorithms, and machine intelligence—which includes your points of social pressure and manipulation. And then they sell it.

- The more data they get, the more accurate predictive analysis becomes, and the more profit it generates for Facebook.
- Facebook and Google this quarter did better than they've ever done before, despite all sorts of public attacks, because they're getting more and better data and therefore selling more and better predictive analysis to third parties.
- The greater your data set is, and the more developed your machine intelligence is, the more you're able to develop predictive analysis.

IMAGINE WHAT HAPPENS WHEN A DICTATORSHIP OWNS DATA

Imagine what happens when a dictatorship owns data. Forms of this are now being used by China. *This is actually happening now.*

- ◆ Think about the social control there.
- ◆ Think about how sophisticated artificial intelligence has become.

Therefore, we need to convene the world around a shared new Story based on shared First Values and First Principles.

One of the first questions we need to address when we create global intimacy is: *Who owns the data?* The data can't be owned by private companies in this particular way because *whoever owns the data runs the world.*

If the data is owned by a bunch of private companies, with are owned by about twenty-five people, we have the "conditioners" who are able to run the world despotically.

IN THE ABSENCE OF UNIQUE SELF, SOCIAL SELF BECAME THE ANIMATING ENERGY OF THE NERVOUS SYSTEM OF THE PLANET

What we've done here is diagnosis: **We've identified the mixture of surveillance capitalism with its profit and power agenda, together with utopianism—Skinner and Pentland responding to existential risk. That utopianism being adopted by the founders of the major players in the tech plex, who are all surveillance capitalists. And all of them are postmodern, that is to say without First Values and First Principles.**

Although he died before postmodernism really took hold, Skinner was actually an early postmodernist. Skinner was a behaviorist and a materialist, who basically said, *interiority is off the table.* He was not a bad guy, and he was a beautiful utopian. *Walden Two* is a beautiful book. Skinner himself stood for value, but he just thought that value was socially constructed, because with his view of universal values, he said, *there's no way to articulate that.* He rejected C.S. Lewis's natural law. And he was partly right in rejecting it; Lewis's natural law actually didn't understand evolution.

I'm sure that Skinner would have loved our notion of evolving First Principles and First Values, and I'm sure he would have come on board in that, and I think he could have come on board on with a notion of True Self and Unique Self. But those models didn't exist in society during his time. The only model that existed was separate self.

So, Skinner says, *We have to move beyond the freedom and dignity of the separate self*—not because he was a bad guy, like Zuboff says—but because he didn't have a sense of Unique Self, so he could only go to social self. **So partly through his influence, the social self became the animating energy of the nervous system of the planet.**

OUR JOB IS TO ENGAGE IN A RECONSTRUCTIVE PROJECT OF VALUE SO WE CAN MUSTER THE NECESSARY OUTRAGE AGAINST THE TECH PLEX

So what's our job? We're going to evolve the source code of culture and consciousness, and evolving the source code of culture and consciousness is the evolution of love. What we've tried to do here is crack open here literally what's going on all the way on the inside; what's animating the Tech Plex.

Here's the paradox: **Shoshana Zuboff gets exactly half of it.** In other words, she's horrified at the tech plex. She does a magisterial job of detailing sixteen different structures of surveillance capitalism. But she doesn't understand the following critical points:

1. She pretty much ignores the objective existential risk that we're facing, and only mentions it a couple of times.
2. She herself has stepped out of the Field of Value. So she gets really angry at the tech plex, but she can't root her anger at the tech plex in First Values and First Principles because she's speaking a kind of postmodern story, rooted in modernity, which says that value, including the value of the individual, is at best a social construction—but it's not more than that.

Paradoxically, Zuboff says that *it's really important to name surveillance capitalism because only if we name it can we actually transform it*—but she won't name First Principles and First Values.

So, she says, *I'm going to arouse astonishment and outrage when people realize what surveillance capitalism is doing.* **But you can only be genuinely outraged when you experience that there's an *actual* violation of value— objective value, real value, not socially constructed value.**

If value is just fiction, then maybe the social self is the best way to go. It's only when you get the First Value and First Principle of personhood and uniqueness that you're truly outraged.

The reason Zuboff doesn't adopt First Values and First Principles is because she doesn't have a conception of it. She thinks all there is natural law, which was dismissed by the Academy, so *the best we have is the old liberal order.* But here's the deal, **postmodernity took down the old liberal order.** Throughout her book, she refers to the liberal values of individuality, but postmodernity took those down entirely; that's all been thoroughly deconstructed. **So we have to now engage in a reconstructive project.**

It's only in a post-postmodern reconstructive project, in which there's a set of evolving First Values and First Principles, that we can actually muster the outrage that Zuboff magisterially and gorgeously seeks to invoke.

But without First Values and First Principles, we don't know why we should be outraged that Google has decided that it owns our data. It's not against the law. It was unprecedented in 2000 when Google decided to mine the data exhaust of our web participation and then realized that that data exhaust would be converted by machine intelligence into a text and sold to third parties. **It wasn't against the law. It wasn't against anything**

except for First Values and First Principles. But no one had articulated First Values and First Principles, because postmodernity said *it's all a social construction of reality.*

So paradoxically, Zuboff herself is, in some subtle sense, allied and aligned with the overlords of the tech plex, whom she attacks—because both of them refuse to embrace First Values and First Principles.

Zuboff relies on the old liberal order, which is easily explainable as a social construction and as a fiction, while the postmodernists of the tech plex adopt the social self because they don't have any First Principles and First Values, such as uniqueness or personhood.

We're not here to get angry at anyone. We're not here to be outraged at this reality. These are not bad people—these are great people.

But it's our job to actually make the da Vinci move. We're at a time between worlds, a time between stories.

The overwhelming moral imperative for those with eyes to see is to take our seat at the table of history and evolve the source code. For this we need:

- A new narrative of identity
- A new narrative of self
- A new universe story
- A new narrative of communion: not a social hive but a Unique Self Symphony
- Not social self but Unique Self
- Not natural law but evolving First Values and First Principles

INDEX

fundamental, 60, 69, 77, 92, 101, 111, 123, 179, 189, 190, 191, 193, 199, 207

fundamentalist, 14, 127, 212

genes, 167

genius, 50

gifts, 39, 103, 138, 157, 161, 168, 171, 204, 205

Global
coherence, 13, 14, 78, 80, 81, 185
ethos, 68, 82, 108, 121, 127, 148
intimacy, 12, 13, 74, 80, 185, 227
intimacy disorder, 12, 13, 74, 80, 185

Global Action Paralysis, 65

global ethos for a global civilization, 68, 108, 121, 127

Goddess, 14

gorgeousness, 5, 6, 7, 23, 31, 32, 34, 41, 48, 49, 53, 60, 62, 87, 103, 117, 129, 138, 151, 154, 157, 160, 169, 171, 181, 195, 229

greatness, 38, 152, 180, 181

ground, 10, 35, 37, 121, 127, 132, 148, 149, 152, 185, 209

Hamilton, Diane, 32

Harari, Yuval Noah, 67, 224

Harris, Sam, 9

Hasidic, 22, 160

heart, 11, 12, 14, 20, 27, 39, 43, 55, 63, 111, 112, 114, 121, 124, 127, 129, 131, 132, 133, 137, 146, 147, 149, 162, 163, 180, 185, 202

heaven, 120, 146

Hebrew, 10, 22, 23, 65, 109, 114, 124, 136, 157, 158, 159, 166, 193, 194
wisdom, 65

hero, 63

hierarchy, 61

Holy of Holies, 115, 116

Homo amor, 31, 33, 34, 35, 36, 37, 38, 63, 70, 96, 114, 115, 127, 134, 135, 143, 149, 150, 152, 153, 154, 156, 168, 173, 180, 195, 224, 225

Homo sapiens, 63, 90, 104, 114, 127, 135, 156, 224

honor, 32, 67, 96, 103, 121

Hubbard, Barbara Marx, 124

human, 5, 6, 8, 10, 15, 16, 17, 18, 19, 20, 26, 30, 34, 36, 40, 44, 45, 47, 60, 63, 65, 67, 69, 72, 73, 74, 75, 76, 79, 80, 82, 83, 85, 87, 90, 93, 94, 95, 101, 108, 118, 119, 120, 123, 126, 127, 130, 131, 135, 136, 140, 142, 150, 155, 156, 172, 176, 177, 178, 179, 180, 183, 184, 185, 186, 187, 193, 196, 201, 202, 206, 207, 208, 209, 210, 211, 212, 213, 214, 215, 216, 219, 220, 223, 224, 225

humanity, 7, 11, 75, 78, 156, 176, 212

humans, 155, 172, 175, 183, 184, 215

I-Am, 37

identity, 6, 7, 9, 16, 26, 27, 31, 35, 36, 44, 66, 68, 73, 74, 78, 80, 102, 127, 177, 186, 188, 209, 210, 221, 230

illusion, 26, 38, 181, 210, 221

mathematics, 135, 155, 175, 176, 215

McIntosh, Steve, 129

Mead, Margaret, 129, 130

meditation, 22, 43, 44, 56, 76, 85, 102, 176

me experience, 62

memory, 12, 13, 142, 147, 163, 166, 168

memory of the future, 12, 13, 142, 147, 166

mind, 18, 33, 34, 35, 44, 53, 56, 57, 114, 136, 147, 155, 156, 158, 177, 178, 180, 186, 202

miracle, 151, 197

model, 3, 27, 89, 94, 112, 213, 214, 219, 222, 224, 228

modern, 9, 18, 22, 29, 34, 38, 46, 61, 64, 65, 67, 74, 194, 214

modernity, 8, 9, 15, 17, 21, 35, 61, 66, 73, 74, 76, 79, 81, 84, 86, 87, 130, 228

mother, 11, 139

multi-cell, 33

music, 50, 70, 155

Myers-Briggs, 100

mystery, 46, 49, 64, 184

mystic, 21, 22

mysticism, 8, 12, 13, 22, 25, 26, 27, 53, 102, 145, 146, 159, 166, 190

Nachman of Breslov, 147

New Age, 14, 196

new human, 35, 36, 120, 134, 135, 156

new humanity, 35, 36, 70, 120, 134, 135, 156

new Story, 9, 10, 14, 15, 64, 65, 68, 73, 77, 82, 107, 108, 112, 116, 121, 127, 130, 132, 148, 150, 152, 185, 227

new Story of Value, 130, 150

noosphere, 34, 44

now-ing, 163

ontological, 176, 177, 183

Ord, Toby, 4, 9, 40

otherness, 44, 188

Outrageous Acts of Love, 40, 41

Outrageous Love, 29, 30, 31, 35, 41, 102, 115, 129, 130, 131, 132, 133, 134, 149, 172, 173, 181, 198

Outrageous Love Letters, 102, 172

Page, Larry, 93, 96, 104, 217, 226

pandemic, 11, 12, 60, 61, 72, 77, 81, 112

paradox, 108, 109, 224, 228, 230

partial, 38, 85, 86, 139, 141, 202, 219, 220

particles, 19, 46, 54, 74, 177, 186

particular, 16, 23, 46, 49, 64, 84, 85, 87, 89, 90, 91, 94, 101, 114, 121, 145, 154, 157, 159, 170, 177, 187, 188, 190, 193, 195, 196, 197, 198, 222, 227

pathological, 55

pathos, 44, 187, 188

pattern, 111, 135, 139, 140, 141, 158, 167, 191, 196

peace, 2, 3, 4, 8

Pentecost, 66

Pentland, Alex, 215, 217

Peterson, Jordan, 9

Volume 25 — First Values and First Principles

LIST OF EPISODES

www.ingramcontent.com/pod-product-compliance
Lightning Source LLC
Chambersburg PA
CBHW031148270326
41931CB00006B/188

9 798888 340523